"The relationship we have with ourselves is the most important one of all and affects all our other relationships. If any relationships in your life have you walking on eggshells, this book is a must-read. Even if they don't, Ted's story is one we can all relate to on some level. And the book ends with a message of hope."

—George Allen

HEALTHY ME, HAPPY WE

Healthy Me, Happy We

Transforming Relationships with Yourself and Others

Ted Smith

Published by Mandala Tree Press
www.mandalatreepress.com

Paperback ISBN: 978-1-954801-05-9
Hardcover ISBN: 978-1-954801-07-3
eBook ISBN: 978-1-954801-06-6

SEL021000 SELF-HELP / Motivational & Inspirational
SEL016000 SELF-HELP / Personal Growth / Happiness
FAM000000 FAMILY & RELATIONSHIPS / General

Cover design by Lisa Barbee
Edited by Jessica Ellingson
Typeset by Kaitlin Barwick

DEDICATION

I dedicate this book to my inner child, young Teddy.
You have a tough road ahead, little buddy, but we'll get through
it together. And dude, once the most painful challenges have passed
and you begin to embrace them and who you truly are,
your life will be friggin' awesome.

INTENTION SETTING

May this book find whoever needs its words—
and may it guide, inform, and inspire you
to live a happy, healthy life.

CONTENTS

INTRODUCTION

Are you happy?

I mean *truly* happy.

Do you even know what true happiness feels like? Some people don't. But how can we know what we don't have?

If you answered my first question as yes—and you truly mean it with confidence—that's wonderful news. And you could probably set the book down right now.

On the other hand, if you initially answered yes, is it possible you are just deluding yourself? Are you trying to convince yourself that you're happy—because who would want to admit that they're unhappy? Studies show that humans are more willing to convince themselves of pleasure than of pain—we don't want to believe we're unhappy, so we convince ourselves we're happy when we're really not. Unhappiness is certainly not a fun place to be—especially when we're realizing the reality of it for the first time.

Remember that you're the only one reading this right now, so you're safe to contemplate the truth of your current situation. You don't have to worry about answering these questions in a way that placates other people.

If the answer is that you're not happy right now (or that you could be happier), that's okay—I'm going to help lead you to a place where you can find happiness again (or perhaps for the first time). But no more lying to yourself about where you currently are. It's not doing you any favors. And it certainly won't do you any good during this discussion we're about to have.

Next question: If you can admit that you're unhappy, do you know why? Or perhaps the question should be, *can you admit why?* Chances are you already know the answer.

For the longest time, I was unhappy but did not know why—or at least, I did not want to admit to myself what that reason was. The two most important relationships in my life at the time were unhealthy—the one I had with my ex-partner of fifteen years and the one I had with myself. Both of these relationships needed significant attention.

If you're unhappy, what's stopping you from changing that? If your answer is that the people, places, or things around you need to change, I have a reality check for you: while external circumstances and relationships may influence where you are today, they are not what's in your way. Only one person is holding you back from finding happiness. Can you guess who that might be? (*Psst*. Check the mirror.)

That being said, sometimes the people we're around or the environments we find ourselves in are unhealthy. Because we can't necessarily expect others to change, we may need to take matters into our own hands to change our external circumstances before we can even begin to look inward.

Another question: Would the eight-year-old version of yourself be proud, happy, and excited to become who you are now? Or would that little kid feel worried, scared, or sad to see what you've become and how you feel about yourself? How do you feel about your answer to this question?

And the final question (for now): Are you really okay settling for unhappiness? Or do you want to finally do something about it—and make that eight-year-old proud, happy, and excited to become you?

> "You are what you settle for."
>
> —JANIS JOPLIN—

Too many people settle for a life in which they are unhappy. Whether they hate their jobs, are single and lonely, or are stuck in a loveless (or even hateful) romantic relationship, these people have resigned themselves to lives where they lack passion, purpose, joy, energy, or sometimes even the will to carry on. They think, "Who am I to be happy?"

Everyone on this planet is worthy of being happy. That includes you.

I'm not here to give you career advice, though in my experience, finding happiness within ourselves allows all aspects of our lives—career, finance, mind, body, spirit, and relationships—to fall into place. So who knows—perhaps if you're unhappy in your career, this book may help with that, too.

My focus will be on relationships—both with others and with the self. It all begins with ourselves, but sometimes it's difficult to start there if we're trying to deal with challenging relationships that require more of our time and energy than is healthy. That was the case for me; ultimately, I had to end my fifteen-year relationship because the toxicity impeded my ability to have a healthy relationship with myself.

Those debilitating, all-consuming challenges we may experience with others can include abuse and addiction, both of which I experienced in my past relationship. While we can experience abuse and addiction in combination with each other (as I did), they can also occur separately.

I want to forewarn you that the first two chapters in this book may be triggering, upsetting, or otherwise uncomfortable for you to read, depending on the experiences you have had in relationships. *Be sure to create a safe space for yourself as you read through the challenges I faced.* For example, if you've been through some shit, I wouldn't recommend reading the first half of the book in a public place. Some uncomfortable emotions may come up, and you want to be in a place where you can freely feel them without worrying about who's around you. In addition, if the material gets too heavy or overwhelmingly relatable, feel free to set the book down and come back to it later (but I recommend that you *do* come back to it later—*especially* if it hits you hard, because that means this book was meant to reach you). *Just remember that you are in control of your own journey here.*

Another fair warning: because I have your best interests at heart, I'm not going to sugarcoat this stuff. I'm going to give it to you straight (even though I'm a big ol' homo). This may mean that, at times, it feels like I'm in your face. Just know that it comes from a place of love. I want you to be happy.

While my relationship was unquestionably toxic, it didn't necessarily start out that way—which is often true for other toxic relationships as well. The red flags associated with abuse and addiction are plentiful. One of the reasons I'm writing this book is to help you recognize these unhealthy behaviors—both the obvious and the subtle—as early on as possible so that you don't have to suffer like I did.

I'm here to share my story in case it's helpful to you. If there are aspects that resonate with you about the unhealthy relationships I experienced with my ex-husband or with myself, I urge you to get help. My intent here is to give you a starting point to help you recognize the issues you may be experiencing but haven't identified yet. Then it's up to you to take the next steps.

My goal in sharing my experience is neither to vilify my ex nor proclaim my victimhood but instead to help you identify any potentially similar characteristics in your own relationship(s). "Relationship(s)" is possibly plural here because the characteristics of unhealthy relationships extend beyond romantic partnerships and can be found in relationships with family, friends, and coworkers as well.

We learn by contrast, thus the reason I am starting with an explanation of unhealthy relationships—so you understand what not to do. My story is a bit extreme, and it's possible your experiences have been nowhere near as challenging. However, if aspects of your own relationships resonate with what I describe, this awareness could be the first step to making your life more manageable and enjoyable.

I'll also cover the challenges in my relationship with myself because, as it turns out, the relationship with the self is damn important in how we relate to other people. Following that, I'll describe what the healing journey can look like for those of us who must recover from unhealthy relationships with others and begin creating a healthy relationship with ourselves. Finally, I'll get into what healthy relationships look like—again, with others and with the self—to contrast against unhealthy relationships. Always good to end on a positive note. And I want to make sure you put this book down with a feeling of hope that things can get better.

I'm not a therapist. This book is not meant to be a tool for therapy. Instead, think of this book as a conversation with a friend—a coach who can help you recognize the unhealthy aspects of your relationships. It's possible you are where I was—at least to some degree—so allow me to share what worked for me and what didn't. My story of survival, healing, and transformation is meant to encourage and guide you to do the same in your own life.

We're all the protagonists of our own stories. And I think we often forget that the people around us who impact our lives (whether positively or negatively) are also the protagonists of *their* own stories. This means we are all self-centered to a degree, but this is not necessarily a bad thing. In fact, when we experience our own transformation and healing, the relationships outside ourselves will also change for the better.

The egoic concept that we are the center of our own universe absolutely impacts our relationships with other people. We may think that others' words and actions are what cause our behaviors and reactions, but really, it's our own thoughts that cause our emotions and feelings. And our thoughts and perspectives are based on our previous experiences. Two people could experience the exact same scenario, but because they each had different experiences leading up to that moment, one might be happy while the other is upset.

> "Most experiences are both good and bad, at the same time. What changes is our perspective."
>
> —MARK MANSON—

When past wounds trigger and upset us in the present, we need to heal the wounds—which we do by feeling our feelings. This is part of the journey we'll take together as well. (And if you're thinking, "Feeling our feelings? What the hell does that mean?"—don't worry, I'll explain.)

Plus, some people are just generally happier individuals who are less upset by everyday events—usually because they've done the work on themselves to feel inner peace and joy regardless of what's going on around them. My goal is to direct you toward becoming one of those people, but that means you've got some work to do, just as I did (and do).

However, becoming a generally happier person does not mean you will feel good all the time. That would be unhealthy, not to mention impossible. I want to set that expectation now so that you don't look forward to a life free from all pain. Those less pleasurable feelings of sadness, anger, and fear will still surface—but that's a good thing. Our feelings give us information and feedback on what's working and not working for us.

I'm a huge proponent of the phrase, "Everything happens for a reason." I believe the universe gives us challenging situations to face so that we can learn and grow. Our biggest challenges usually become a big part of our identity because they shape who we are as human beings.

While we may all be the protagonists of our own stories, that doesn't mean we're the heroes of our own stories—at least not yet. However, I'm here to help steer you toward that place. You can be your own hero. And you can be grateful for the challenges you've faced. But it'll take some work to recognize the issues in your current life and learn how to change them for the better.

SETTING THE STAGE

Just a couple of years ago, I had zero concept of what true happiness was. To help you understand the journey that led me to write this book, allow me to paint a picture of a typical day in the life of my fifteen-year relationship. Any given weeknight with my ex-husband would look something like the following scenario.

The workday is over, so it's time for a drink. Whether the reason is to de-stress or celebrate something—or merely because it's what we do every day—it's time for a drink. The evening starts amicably, perhaps chatting while he begins cooking dinner and we enjoy our cocktails.

Within a few minutes, my stomach tightens. *Oh, shit,* I think. *I better find something productive to do so he doesn't yell at me. I can't just stand here.* I feed the cats and clean their litter boxes. I give an outward appearance of efficiency to him, but in reality, I do these tasks as slowly as possible to fill the time until dinner is ready. Because I know the energy in the room can change quickly, I know that being in a different room is safe . . . to a point. I take a moment to watch the cats gobble up their dinner while chuckling a bit as they purr in between chews. Then, a moment of envy, wishing I could also have a life so simple.

My heart stops. *Now I probably need to do something in the kitchen so he doesn't think I'm avoiding him. But it's gotta be something where I won't be in his way. I need to remember to grab the wine out of the freezer when dinner's almost ready because he'll get mad if I forget—but we're not at that point yet, I don't think.*

The tension in my stomach releases momentarily as I think of something. *I know, I'll fix us a shot.*

We down the bourbon, and I feel it warm my throat and stomach. Things are going well. We're getting along. Soon, my smile fades. This time, it's my chest that tightens. *Okay, gotta keep moving. I'll get the TV ready for dinner.* This takes all of about ten seconds, and then I'm once again at a loss of how to fill the time. *Come on, Ted—you've gotta be able to think of something.*

I watch him rush around the kitchen with urgency from one task to the next. Cooking is important business—and something I don't understand. Garlic, onion, and various herbs and spices fill the air with anticipatory flavor. "It smells so good!" I say, knowing that the compliment is necessary. If I don't say it now, I'll hear about it later.

He ignores me and keeps shuffling, but that doesn't bother me too much. *Not a problem*, I think—*at least we're still getting alo—*

"Don't worry, I'll get it," he grumbles as he yanks open the freezer door, pulls out a bottle of white wine, and hurriedly sets it on the counter. *Dammit*, I think. *How was I supposed to know dinner was almost ready? He didn't say anything.* And if I asked, he would perceive it as impatient, ungrateful, or more obvious that I know nothing about cooking. *I had to keep quiet for my own good then, but I'm paying for it now.*

"Can you at least grab the wine glasses?" he barks. Our time of getting along is over. *Well, that didn't last long. Here we go again.* I rush to fetch the wine glasses as quickly as possible to show him I acknowledge the importance of it. Meanwhile, he opens the bottle, slams the corkscrew on the counter, and returns to finishing up the food. The gesture doesn't include words, but I know exactly what he's thinking—I don't know how to use the type of corkscrew he's using, and he's showing me just how easy it is. *I'm so stupid.*

7

He trips over one of the cats and screams in frustration. I wince. "I need another shot," he says in defeat. I hurry to pour it. *Better make one for myself, too, or he'll be even more pissed.*

I bring the shot glasses over while he plates our food. I stand by him, waiting patiently. "Don't just stand there. I hate it when you do that," he snarls. I turn around and take a few steps to give him some space. My heart is in my stomach. I don't know what to do to make him happy.

Finally, he's ready for the shot. I raise my glass and say a simple, "I love you," with a pleading tone to it. He quickly returns, "Love you, too," rolling his eyes without meeting mine and then downs the shot.

We sit down for dinner. He heaves a sigh. "I'm sorry," he says calmly. "That was just really frustrating. I asked you to get the wine ready—it's the one thing I asked you to do."

"I know. I'm sorry," I reply. *Please let this just be it.*

"I just wanna have fun with you tonight. Can we start over?" he asks.

The tightness in my stomach, neck, and back subsides. I stifle my own sigh of relief. "Yes, let's do that."

Thank God. I got off easy this time.

OKAY, THE STAGE IS SET— NOW WHAT?

I had no idea how toxic and abusive this relationship was. This was just another night in the life. It was all I knew. I did the best I could with what I had in front of me.

But there were so many ways that situation could have been handled better—by both of us. We weren't even drunk yet, though that was well on its way, and that would only make things worse.

Within the story, you likely perceived an obvious external abuse component, but my internal thought process was also unhealthy. Notice how some of the only things I say out loud are "I love you" (in a pleading, almost desperate manner) and "I'm sorry" (when there's not really anything for me to apologize for). Everything else is an internal dialogue of abusing myself, doubting myself, feeling frustration toward him, anticipating what's coming next, or pleading to escape the present moment.

The cycle of abuse would continue through the night after the snippet I shared here, with escalated abuse both externally and internally as the drinks continued to go down the hatch. On top of that, my ex's alcohol addiction had severe short-term and long-term health impacts that did a number on both of us and added another complex layer to the emotional abuse and codependency.

My life was a constant state of hyperawareness, anticipation, dread, and fear—and that created a complete inability to be present, as well as complex trauma from which I'm still recovering. I'm here to share that story, as well as answer the question I'm guessing you're asking of why the hell I stayed in that relationship for fifteen years.

After a decade and a half of challenges, I'm now on a journey of healing. I have a much better idea of what a healthy relationship looks like, both externally and internally. And if you can relate to any aspects of the story I shared above or the experiences I'm about to share, I'm also here to help you understand what I've learned about healthy relationships so that you can begin to experience them yourself.

WAIT—IS THIS BOOK FOR ME OR NOT?

Maybe you've never experienced abuse or addiction in your relationships. Should you read on?

I recommend that you do. A few thoughts here:

1. Maybe you think you've never experienced these issues in your relationships when they are (or were), in fact, present. I can help you identify them. And I expect there will be points throughout the first half of the book where you can relate to my experiences to some degree.
2. Abuse can be more subtle than you may realize.

3. Addiction does not have to just include chemical addictions like drugs and alcohol. We can also (or instead) be addicted to behaviors—and even to other people.

4. There's a good chance that someone close to you has experienced or is currently experiencing a relationship that involves abuse or addiction. If you worry about how these loved ones are doing and wonder what might be going on behind closed doors, this book may provide some insights that can help you help them.

There may also be points in the next couple of chapters where you think, "Wait, I thought this book was supposed to be about happiness? This is some heavy shit." Fair warning—the road to finding happiness can be a rough one, and this book follows that path. You've gotta go through some stuff first. But trust me—it's all worth the journey.

> "The best way out is always through."
>
> —ROBERT FROST—

The second half of this book can serve anyone. Even if your life up until this point has not had a ton of pain and trauma, we all have stuff from which we need to heal in order to have healthy relationships with ourselves and with others. As you're about to learn, *a healthy me allows for a happy we.*

ABUSE

Disclaimer: As a reminder, the following two chapters may contain experiences that are triggering or otherwise uncomfortable for you. Make sure to give yourself a safe, loving space as you read further.

Usually, we are our own worst critics. But when it comes to abuse, that is not necessarily the case.

My previous relationship of fifteen years involved emotional, mental, sexual, financial, and physical abuse. But when I was actively in the relationship, I didn't realize this. I knew I was unhappy, and I knew I didn't like how he treated me—but I didn't know that what was happening was considered abuse.

The same might be true for you. I'm here to help you recognize those signs and symptoms of an abusive relationship. Awareness of your current situation is the first key step to transforming your life.

In this chapter, we'll discuss what I've learned about the various forms of abuse, including things that surprised me, things I did not initially understand. We'll talk about why abused people seem to have blinders on that prevent them from noticing red flags and getting out of a relationship that is unsafe and all kinds of problematic. Finally, we'll talk about what to ultimately do about these relationships.

Before we get started, I have a question for you: When you think of abuse, what comes to mind? I suggest pausing here for a moment to give that some thought (*before* "cheating" by reading ahead!).

Your answers to the question might include things like putting some-one down, name-calling, threatening, physical assault, rape, and invok-ing fear. You may have also answered from the target's standpoint and thought of crying, shaking, cowering, and shutting down. All of these answers are correct—but there are many additional layers to abuse.

My ex is a narcissist—something else I didn't fully understand until the last few months of our relationship. I always thought a narcissist was just someone who is extremely self-absorbed—which is true—but there's so much more to it than that. Narcissism is characterized by an excessive need for admiration, disregard for others' feelings, an inability to handle any criticism, and a sense of entitlement.[1]

There is a spectrum of narcissism, sociopathy, and psychopathy that I could explain—but at the end of the day, the psychological terminol-ogy doesn't matter. What matters is how you feel and how this behavior can impact you. I've included a list of resources at the back of this book that go in-depth on the characteristics of each abusive personality type and what people experience in relationships with these individuals. This information was critical in my own journey to validate my experience.

To say a relationship with a narcissist, sociopath, or psychopath is draining would be one hell of an understatement. These abusers can remove your entire sense of self and beat everything out of you until all that remains is a shell of a human being. Not every day involves a blow-up argument, but every day does include abuse, whether it be subtle or overt.

Not all abusers have to be narcissists, sociopaths, or psychopaths; these are just the most extreme examples. Some people are just ass-holes! (Interestingly, not all narcissists are abusive, either—but those individuals are rare.) Rudeness, disrespect, condescension, manipula-tion, sarcasm, teasing, hurtfulness, spitefulness, and general meanness do not constitute abuse if they occur in rare, isolated incidents—but when they occur repeatedly and in combination with each other, the patterns become abusive.

1. "Narcissistic Personality Disorder," Mayo Clinic, accessed February 1, 2021, https://www.mayoclinic.org/diseases-conditions/narcissistic-personality-disorder/symptoms-causes/syc-20366662.

It's important to point out that every relationship is slightly different. I'm not saying that all abusive relationships will mirror my exact experience. Many abused people, myself included, read about narcissists and other abusers—or see extreme versions of them in television and movies—and think, "Well, this isn't *exactly* like what I'm experiencing—so my partner must not actually be abusive. They must not be a narcissist/sociopath/psychopath like I thought. It's probably all in my head. I've got it easier than other people do, and I should be grateful for what I have."

Trust your gut. If you feel like something is off, you're probably right.

And keep an open mind as you read through the next couple of chapters. My version of things may seem extreme, but there is a spectrum to how unhealthy a relationship can be. Thus, if you can relate to certain aspects of my experience, take note, and then continue learning more about relationships with these types of individuals.

Remember, abuse doesn't only happen in romantic partnerships. It's just as common with family, with friends, and in professional relationships. And perhaps you think it would be easy to identify abuse on your own, but you might be surprised.

For example, do you find yourself putting more emotional energy into relationships with certain people than what seems reasonable? Abused people often find that 90 percent of our energy goes into the most toxic people in our lives (as if it's a full-time job), leaving only 10 percent for everyone else. We are obsessed with trying to make that "90 percent relationship" work by constantly either doing things to make the person happy or working to resolve one or more of many ongoing conflicts.

If that "90 percent relationship" is with your partner, it may seem normal to exert that much energy into the person with whom you spend most of your time. It's not. In healthy relationships, we can give our full attention to the task or people at hand when we're not with our partners (e.g., at work, with friends, or even just with ourselves). But in abusive relationships, our partners largely consume our thoughts, feelings, and energy, regardless of whether we're with them.

If you are frequently upset by things your partner says or does or about your relationship in general, there is probably some important work to do on yourself and your relationship. (You may think it's all on your partner to change their behavior, but that's out of your control.) If you feel alone in your relationship or that your relationship is impacting and distracting you from other aspects of your life like work or getting daily activities done, it's time we do something about it. The first step is being able to recognize when things feel off or aren't going well and identify the reasons.

WHAT DOES ABUSE LOOK LIKE?

I think we all have some understanding of what emotional, mental, sexual, and physical abuse entail. However, there were several aspects of abuse that I did not comprehend until the last few months of my relationship when I began to see a therapist.

First, emotional abuse does not mean constant ridicule and fighting. Instead, there is a cycle of abuse:

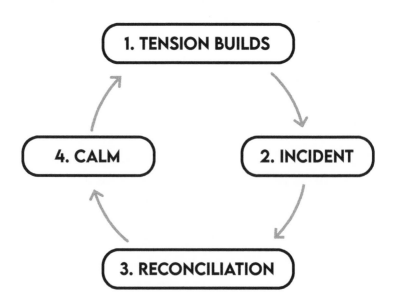

While tension and stress build, the abuser may begin to feel wronged, neglected, or ignored and respond by accusing, yelling, or demanding unrealistic expectations of the abused. Meanwhile, the abused—having been through the cycle many times by this point—is anxiously, fearfully walking on eggshells to avoid upsetting the abuser.

The "incident" occurs with the peak of verbal, physical, or sexual abuse. This is usually prompted by something the abused says or does, which often seems insignificant and undeserving of such a reaction.

Next, the two reconcile. The abuser often does some combination of promising the abuse will never happen again, showering the abused with gifts, and giving a back-handed apology—for example, "I didn't want to hurt you, but I just get so frustrated by how you don't listen to me" (or "don't understand me" or "don't do _____ the way it has to be done"). The abused, meanwhile, feels relief that the peak of the abuse has passed while simultaneously feeling pain, sadness, humiliation, disrespect, and fear.

When I was learning about abuse, the most surprising yet most important stage was the calm, also known as the "love-bombing" stage, in which the abuser showers the abused with affection and love and is a pleasure to be around. *Including this stage in the cycle is imperative to keeping the target engaged in the relationship.* The abused believes the good times will continue, and in times of strife, they latch onto the memories of previous love bombs and look forward to future love bombs. And in many cases (mine included), this stage prevents the target from realizing that what is happening is considered abuse.

In addition to the above cycle, there were several other aspects of abuse I did not initially understand:

1. **Emotional abuse can be subtle and not always involve words.** In fact, it can be just the opposite—in the form of silent treatment or a facial expression that appears threatening, angry, or otherwise ominous.
2. **Financial abuse is a thing.** I didn't even know this concept existed. Financial abuse involves controlling a target's ability to acquire, use, and maintain financial resources. This is more common than you may realize; a study by the Centers for

Financial Security found that 99 percent of domestic violence cases also involved financial abuse.[2]

3. **Sexual abuse does not only include assault and rape.** Among other things, it can also include engaging in or being forced to engage in sexual behavior that does not make you feel comfortable. In addition, sexual abuse can also include emotionally abusive acts in the context of sex.

4. **Physical abuse does not only include violence.** It can include acts of intimidation, such as seemingly playful things like tickling or wrestling. Abusers can use tactics like this to subtly let the abused know that the abuser can overpower them.

5. **As implied above, playfulness and abuse are not mutually exclusive.** In fact, abusers often purposely mask what they're doing by being playful so that when the abused reacts, the abuser can make them feel crazy or oversensitive for attacking something that was "just a joke" or "just playing around."

6. **Domestic abusers often don't hit.** In fact, the likely reason many of them never hit their partners is they know it won't be tolerated. For some reason, hitting is the one form of abuse that many people can immediately recognize as abuse. Other forms of abuse may be tolerated for a long time—sometimes, unfortunately, for a lifetime. And I believe this tolerance often has to do with not recognizing what's happening as abuse.

7. **Emotional abuse tends to be the overarching type of abuse across all these categories.** For example, there is emotional abuse involved in sexually abusive acts. And one category often overlays with others as well, like how emotional abuse impacts one's thinking (i.e., mental abuse).

For me personally, these were eye-openers. Not recognizing these signs played a big role in keeping me in the dark—not recognizing that what was happening was abuse.

2. Sherri Gordon, "How to Identify Financial Abuse in a Relationship," Very Well Mind, last modified May 2, 2020, https://www.verywellmind.com/financial-abuse-4155224.

COMMON TRAITS
OF ABUSERS

In order to help you identify abuse, let's talk about some characteristics abusers often exemplify. As we do, allow me to put you in the shoes of the abused in these examples.

Self-hatred. One core problem with certain types of narcissists, sociopaths, and psychopaths is that they loathe themselves. This may surprise you because these individuals often act as if they love themselves to a toxic degree—but you are likely confusing love with obsession. All they can think about is themselves, and because they hate themselves, they are filled with hate.

The absence of love for themselves makes it impossible for them to love anyone else. Their abusive actions are often projecting their own lack of self-worth and the things they hate about themselves onto those around them. Abusers crave intimacy and fear being alone, but their words and actions sabotage themselves by repelling those around them.

> "If you can't love yourself, how the hell are you gonna love somebody else?"
>
> —RUPAUL—

After leaving my ex, I recognized that because he was unable to love himself, he was unable to love me. I was hurt and saddened by this and felt like our entire relationship was a lie.

However, I realized soon after that I also was never really in love with him; instead, *I was in love with his potential.* I believed (and still believe) he could do incredible things with his life in terms of career, creative hobbies, and even being a good partner in our relationship if he would just get the help he needed and applied himself. *But attaching ourselves to a version of someone else that doesn't exist is not healthy, nor is it in tune with reality.*

In order to truly love someone, we have to love who they are in the present. At the same time, true love of others also requires loving ourselves. I was definitely lacking in this area—nowhere near the level of self-hatred that my ex felt toward himself, but I definitely had some work to do on loving myself.

Masterful perceptiveness. Abusers are incredibly perceptive—almost frighteningly so. They pick up on the areas about which you feel most self-conscious and use that to their advantage. For me, I was hyper-sensitive to being called stupid, so my ex would do this on multiple occasions, no matter how many times I asked him to stop. I was also self-conscious about my appearance, and he would criticize me about my posture and belly—sometimes in front of other people. Of course, these were two areas where he was also self-conscious about himself, so this was probably projection on his part as well.

Ignoring boundaries. Abusers push, ignore, and completely anni-hilate boundaries—the points at which we no longer accept others' behavior. In the example above, when I asked my ex to refrain from calling me stupid, his continuation of the behavior was a form of bla-tant disrespect in more ways than one. An important red flag for you to watch out for is if you repeatedly ask someone to change their hurtful behavior and they continue.

Dismissiveness. My ex regularly ignored or interrupted me when I had things to share. At home, he dismissed what I had to say. At gath-erings, when I would tell a story, he would display impatience—either overtly (saying out loud that the story was taking too long) or covertly (with a look that only I could see). Over time, I developed a belief that no one cares what I have to say, which did a number on my self-confidence. When others would interrupt me, I thought they felt the same way he did—that what I had to say wasn't valuable or worth hearing—whether that was their intention or not. Often, I would shut down by either not talking nearly as much or by not talking at all. I still struggle with getting past this issue.

Obsession with self-image. To the outside world, the abuser creates a façade of perfection so no one can see the truth. The abuser may show affection toward you or compliment you (directly or indirectly) in front of other people to give off the impression that they love and appreciate you. It can feel completely foreign because they don't show you that level of affection or talk to you like that when it's just the two of you. The abuser will usually be on their best behavior around other people so that others don't get a clue as to what's happening behind closed doors. Slowly, however, the abuser may introduce abuse for others to observe but ensures that everyone understands this is "normal" and "just how this relationship is."

Possessiveness and isolation from others. This is a big one. Often, the abuser will insist that all relationship problems be discussed between you and them with no outside help from anyone (even professionals). *This is not normal or healthy.* We all need outside opinions and help sometimes. (However, to be clear, the other extreme of someone blasting all their relationship problems to the world around them is also toxic. As with anything, there needs to be balance.)

I believe therapy is a good idea for anyone—not just those with significant mental health issues or other challenges. Someone who doesn't want you discussing your relationship issues outside of the relationship, even in a professional setting, is undoubtedly trying to manipulate and control you.

When it comes to discussing challenges with trusted family and friends, you may feel unable to do this without repercussions from the abuser, or you may be uncomfortable doing this out of embarrassment or fear of having to talk about what's really going on. You may also fear being told something you don't want to hear—i.e., to get out of the relationship. This discomfort with discussing the relationship is a telltale sign that you are not comfortable with the relationship.

We must remember that our trusted family and friends are not our enemies. Even if they tell us something we don't want to hear, we need to remember that they have our best interests at heart. Ultimately, it's up to us to make our own decisions, but sometimes our decision-making abilities are flawed—especially in an abusive relationship.

Maybe you think I'm wrong. From your perspective, it may feel like your relationship with these family and friends (whom you thought you could trust) changed because they don't like your partner, think you could do better, or have concerns about how the relationship has changed you in ways that don't feel right to them. But think about it: If these people were a constant source of love and support in your life until your partner came along, what really changed here—their love for you or your perception of them?

In extreme cases, abusers convince you to distance yourself from your loved ones so they can have you all to themselves. This allows them to manipulate you more easily. You may end up completely cut off from all or most of your family and friends.

Unrealistic demands. Abusive partners also tend to demand an unrealistic, unattainable level of perfection from their partners. Nothing is ever enough to satisfy them. Just when you think you've finally met or exceeded their expectations, there is a demand for more. This can come in relation to various aspects of life—household chores, gifts, sex, praise, attention, and spontaneity to name a few.

Unpredictability. The abusive partner creates an environment for the relationship that is completely unpredictable. Things constantly change at a moment's notice. One minute you're laughing and having a good time; the next minute you're crying because they instigate yet another fight because you "looked at them the wrong way" or said a slightly wrong word. You are walking on eggshells every minute of every day. You are constantly waiting for that other shoe to drop—or, if you're in the midst of yet another argument, you internally beg for it to just be over.

The truth is that while things may seem different from moment to moment, it's really just more of the same but in different forms. *Things are ever-changing yet also never-changing.*

But wait, there's more! Those are a few traits of abusers that I can describe relatively succinctly. Let's dive into some additional aspects of abuse in more detail.

ABUSIVE ARGUMENTS

If an abused person brings up a concern they have with their partner or with the relationship, the discussion will most often lead to an argument or fight. Healthy relationships can (and should) include disagreements as well—but the distinction is in how these differences are handled. In a healthy relationship, there is a back-and-forth discussion of feelings, including active listening, with ultimately resolution or compromise.

In an abusive relationship, on the other hand, the abuser tends to use some combination of the following tactics.

1. **Dismissing you.** The abuser will dismiss your feelings by claiming you are being oversensitive or exaggerating the problem. They may shut down the discussion immediately, possibly by leaving the room or saying something like, "Oh, I'm not dealing with this all over again" or "Oh my God, get over it."

2. **Gaslighting.** The abuser will "gaslight," convincing you that what they said or did never happened—or did not happen the way you perceived it. Abusers are especially good at gaslighting within the midst of the argument by claiming they never said that thing you claimed they said five minutes ago. This tactic leaves you feeling confused, frustrated, and like you might be crazy.

3. **Pushing you to your breaking point.** The abuser will continue to push your buttons within the argument in the hopes of getting an explosive reaction. Returning an abuser's anger with a voice just as loud gives them exactly what they want. That way, your reaction merits an apology. I can't tell you how many times I brought something up as an issue with my ex and ended up being the one to apologize because I got upset during the argument. For me, one of my biggest pet peeves is being interrupted. My ex, knowing this about me, would constantly interrupt me in arguments until I exploded, thus giving him the reaction he wanted so he could turn the blame onto me. *Abusers insist on blaming while remaining blameless.*

> "Your abusive partner doesn't have a problem with his anger; he has a problem with your anger."
>
> —LUNDY BANCROFT—

4. **Dragging it out.** The abuser will purposely drag the argument out to the point that you are exasperated and exhausted. Our fights would sometimes go on for hours. And I lost track of the number of times I escaped to the bathroom to catch myself in the mirror with tear-stained cheeks and red, squinted eyes, begging for it all to just end. (And by that, I don't just mean wanting the

end of the argument—I would often say to my own reflection through the tears, "I just want to die." The arguments were that excruciating, especially after they went on for so long and had happened like that so many times.)

5. **Combining tactics to increase their impact.** All of these tactics, when used successfully and in combination with each other, allow the abuser to avoid having to apologize and own their behavior because the onus falls on you for getting upset in the first place and getting even more upset in the argument. Switching back and forth from the various tactics increases their effectiveness in wearing you down. Ultimately, you will more than likely be the first (and only) one to apologize simply as a mechanism to escape the cycle of the circular argument that goes nowhere. If the abuser apologizes, they don't mean it.

If you find yourself feeling the urge to secretly record your arguments so you can go back and listen to them later to see what went wrong or prove you're not crazy, this is a clear indication that you're being emotionally abused. I recorded several of our fights to try and make sense of them later since I would always be so exasperated by the end of them that I was unclear as to what just happened. "How did it get to this point yet again?" I would think.

Many of the arguments I had with my ex included criticism of my supposed inability to properly communicate. I tended to bottle my emotions and erupt with anger, frustration, and tears at various points throughout the relationship. The problem was that once I vowed to change that behavior and bring up issues as they occurred, doing so would always backfire. When I would bring up my feelings and concerns in a healthy, calm manner, I would be met with the tactics described above, which would make me regret voicing my feelings in the first place and revert back to my old ways of not communicating my feelings at all. My choice to hold back from communicating my feelings (although it didn't feel like I had the choice) caused me to retain blame in our relationship.

Let me pause here and point out that the abusive tactics described above can occur in all sorts of situations, some in isolated incidents that aren't necessarily a continually abusive relationship. Some people occasionally manipulate or gaslight in order to "win" an argument and keep the upper hand. These isolated moments do not necessarily constitute abuse—until they become a pattern. But that doesn't make them right, either.

Generally speaking, the length of arguments with anyone (abusive or not) is often based on how stubborn each person is with respect to being right versus allowing room to see the other person's perspective. However, insisting on being right is often not the healthiest approach—though this can certainly depend on how it's communicated. And in the end, what purpose does it serve to be right? *If you end up "winning" an argument, are you really "winning" if the other person is feeling defeated, hurt, and resentful?*

In my unhealthy relationship, the length of our arguments usually depended on how long it took for *me*—not one of us, just me—to concede, admit he was right (whether I felt that way or not), and apologize (whether I meant it or not).

For the first several years of our relationship, we didn't argue much because I didn't stand up to him. I would just accept his abuse and believe it was all my fault. I remember apologizing to him profusely for being such a "pain in the ass"—when, in reality, I wasn't in the wrong (at least most of the time). I hadn't recognized how baffling and unfair it was for me to be the one apologizing and cowering to his unrealistic and nonsensical demands.

At some point, I decided to try to stand up for myself, but every time I did, his reaction was so negative that I would always regret doing so. Ultimately, it took my giving up for the arguments to end. If you decide to stand up for yourself in discussions with your partner, take note of how your partner reacts to this—especially when you express your feelings calmly and respectfully.

The intensity of the arguments increased under the influence of alcohol, pain, or illness. Alcohol (in either or both of us) only made things worse when it came to trying to have a productive conversation about our relationship. And whenever he was in pain or ill, he would capitalize on these ailments by introducing sympathy and guilt into the mix of manipulative tactics.

For example, he had his wisdom teeth removed and was in pain during recovery. I would wait on him hand and foot, providing comfort as best I could, yet he still called me a "shitty caretaker." And it hurt him to talk, but that didn't stop him from berating me—somehow the pain he experienced from talking was my fault because he had no other option but to tell me what I was doing or saying wrong. Nothing I did was good enough, and rarely would I receive any level of gratitude for taking care of him.

In addition, pain or illness can give an abuser apparent justification for their harmful behavior—it makes sense to both the abuser and abused why they are acting this way. These ailments make them even more irritable and less reasonable.

The repeating pattern of these arguments will lead the target to believe that some things simply can't be done together without leading to a fight. My ex and I couldn't make a damn bed together without fighting. We also couldn't shop together. We would be that couple in the store who everyone's staring at because they're snapping at each other in the middle of aisle 10. My attempts to tone down his volume or intensity in public only made things worse.

I've seen articles and blog posts about how to argue with narcissists, sociopaths, and psychopaths. My best advice can be summarized in one word: *don't*. Just don't. It will not get you anywhere. There is no use wasting your energy.

However, sometimes it's impossible to avoid these arguments—especially when living with the abuser. From my perspective, there are only two ways to get out of an argument:

1. Be the one to apologize.
2. Acknowledge that the abuser is superior to you.

Even if these approaches don't feel right or warranted, it is often the only way to get the abuser off your back. Standing your ground, refusing to apologize, and insisting your way is right (even if this is crystal clear to you) will not get through to the abuser; in fact, it will only drag things out longer.

Narcissists, sociopaths, and psychopaths refuse to (because they are unable to) accept personal responsibility for their words and actions. They cannot and will not admit that they've said or done anything wrong. They may apologize to some degree, but a true apology means changed behavior over the long term, and you will never see this from these types of abusers. (You may see changes in the short term as yet another form of manipulation—the true test is whether the change is more permanent.)

These types of abusers constantly seek power, validation, and superiority over others as their form of self-worth. Feeding their egos and making them believe we feel they are superior will give them exactly what they need. Obviously, this is unhealthy and unfair, but sometimes we have to do what is necessary to survive.

For individuals who choose to remain in these abusive relationships—or more often, feel they have no choice—some have found success using the "grey rock method," in which the abused purposely exhibits no emotion or feeling when the abuser tries to provoke. This strategy aligns with my recommendation to avoid arguments altogether. The lack of reaction leaves the abuser feeling bored, and they will eventually give up. In my (very) limited experience attempting this, I would say it is quite challenging to not react to someone who is verbally attacking and provoking you. But fellow abused individuals have indicated that with practice, it can be effective.

FINANCIAL ABUSE— YES, IT'S A THING

It's 7 a.m. and still dark outside this frigid February morning. A truck engine rumbles, and then I hear the *beep, beep, beep* of it backing up. My heart sinks to my stomach; without even looking, I know exactly what's happening.

I reluctantly approach the window to look outside, and sure as shit, a tow truck is lining itself up with one of our vehicles to haul it away. Three months behind on payments, I immediately know my lending company has had enough. Powerless, I watch my car disappear. Then begins the process of tracking it down, making calls, and driving to pick it up with my tail between my legs.

This was not the first time I had this experience—only the first time, I was lucky enough that the car was parked in a garage that the tow truck driver could not access, and I was able to quickly make a payment online to catch up.

The first time, it was a surprise that the lender took such action. The second time, it was less of a surprise. (See the parallels to emotional abuse?)

Although I always earned a higher-than-average income for my age, I struggled to make ends meet because of poor financial planning and—you guessed it—financial abuse.

Financial abuse is often committed by the primary breadwinner of the relationship—refusing any level of shared income, preventing the abused from working, providing an "allowance" to the abused with strict stipulations about how the money is spent, or withholding money from the abused for even basic expenses like food. This type of abuse traps targets into remaining in the relationship because they cannot provide for themselves or their children on their own. In this sense, financial abuse is arguably one of the most powerful forms of abuse; the target may fully realize the extent of other forms of abuse and know it's in their best interest to end the relationship, but they feel forced to continue in the relationship because of finances.

In my case, on the other hand, I was always the primary breadwinner of our relationship—by a long shot for the majority of those fifteen years. Instead, my ex mismanaged and overspent our money and left me with little say—a form of financial abuse that is different from the norm.

For the first few years of our relationship, I let him have full control of our money since he had a financial background and I trusted him to manage everything responsibly. When we started living together a year and a half into our relationship, he insisted we merge finances with a joint checking account (and no separate accounts) right away. Especially given the fact that I was only nineteen years old at the time, this insistence on his part was a red flag that I didn't recognize because I didn't know any better.

Three years later, I discovered he had stolen over $13,000 from a non-profit organization over the course of nine months. At this point, I realized (the hard way) that I had to start paying more attention to our financial situation. Luckily for him, the board of directors agreed to let him repay the funds instead of pressing charges. However, since I made most of our income, guess who ended up paying most of that money back?

Repayment of that money required me to lie to family to borrow the necessary funds because I couldn't admit what had actually happened. The financial strain caused considerable stress on top of the damage to the relationships involved (ours included) because of what he had done. (At this point, you may be thinking, "Wait, you stayed with him after that?" Yup.)

The financial abuse continued for the remainder of our relationship. Every time I proposed putting together a budget, he scoffed at the idea because he claimed we didn't need one. I'm not sure what the underlying reason for that was—perhaps he saw it as a form of weakness or struggle. Or perhaps he knew a budget would prove his financial irresponsibility, and he certainly didn't want to jeopardize his overspending habits. Whatever the reason, he certainly did not view developing a budget as a fundamental exercise in financial responsibility, which I always thought someone with a background in finance would understand and support.

My company credit card was cancelled three different times due to failure to repay the bills; when I would receive reimbursement for travel expenses charged to that card, the funds would be used for things other than paying off that card. I felt a mix of increased angst and relief with each occurrence because I was honestly surprised my employment status wasn't affected by these infractions (especially the second and third times).

On at least five separate occasions, we had to borrow significant sums of money from family and friends to pay off debt we had accrued but couldn't afford. Requesting these loans was always uncomfortable, and because of continued financial irresponsibility, we often didn't follow the repayment terms of those loans, either. Somehow, the responsibility always fell on me for not only the initial request for funds but also the ongoing requests for reprieves when we failed to repay as agreed.

While I own my part in letting things get that bad and continue that way, I often felt trapped between a rock and a hard place because of the emotional abuse. Asserting the need for financial responsibility was not welcome or even safe; instead, it was easier (at least in the moment) not to speak up against his frivolous purchases of interior décor, clothes, and booze. My denial and avoidance of the issues—much like my approach to other aspects of our relationship—did not serve either one of us. In fact, in the long run, it only made things worse.

Regardless of whether the abuser is the primary breadwinner in the relationship, financial abuse contributes significantly to a target's powerlessness. It is yet another form of control and manipulation. Money may not buy happiness, but it does provide security for basic needs—and when this security is in jeopardy, the target can paradoxically become even more emotionally dependent on the abuser. They rely on the abuser for safety, even though the abuser is primarily responsible for disrupting that safety in the first place.

ABUSE IN THE BEDROOM (GULP)

Then there was the sexual abuse. Like I said, this does not have to mean rape or sexual assault—there are many other layers and different ways to experience it. I'll give you a few examples, which admittedly, are not easy for me to share. But I feel it's important that I do.

One of the earliest red flags in our relationship came when I asked him to get tested for STDs and he refused. I knew he had had unprotected sex with multiple guys before we met, and I also knew it was the safe and responsible thing to do for him to get checked out. He dismissed my concerns, which made me feel stupid and small for bringing them up in the first place. And he never did get tested.

I participated in sexual kinks because I felt they were required to keep him happy and avoid more abuse. I didn't enjoy or feel comfortable taking part in these acts, but I had to be extremely careful about how and when I chose to say no. Often I didn't feel like I had a choice because I knew the level of emotional abuse that was waiting for me on the other side if I tried to say no. So I often obliged.

To this day, well over a year after leaving him, I am still incredibly uncomfortable with the idea of anal sex. The abuse I suffered from him immediately following failed attempts at this was derisive and divisive, which would then get in my head the next time we tried, and it became a vicious cycle. I'll never forget the screaming match we got into about this *on our honeymoon* while drunk and naked in the bedroom. Outside, the beautiful Punta Cana resort had music hopping; guests were talking, laughing, and dancing; a comfortable, warm ocean breeze was beckoning us to come out and experience it—yet we were stuck inside, hashing out yet another blowup. As newlyweds. I can't make this shit up.

My concerns, hesitations, and discomfort with respect to anal sex resulted in his questioning my sexuality. In his mind, anal sex was a requirement in any gay relationship. "And you call yourself a gay man," he would say. The idea that some gay men do not enjoy anal sex was unacceptable and inconceivable to him. And he did not understand that showing compassion and understanding toward my struggles may have been the very thing I needed to feel comfortable and willing to explore this with him. Instead, he shamed me for my feelings, which only furthered the divide between us.

And he did rape me once. For "only" about ten to fifteen seconds, I told him to stop and he kept going. This didn't affect me too much, though, in either the moment or over the long term—and I've realized it's because this type of behavior was so common in the context of our relationship that I don't think of it as some isolated, traumatic event. Just another day in the life.

I'd like to reiterate that your experience may be vastly different. However, just because you haven't been through something as traumatic as rape or assault doesn't mean you haven't experienced sexual abuse. If you've experienced any level of similar discomfort, feelings of uneasiness, unwanted demands, or even trauma when it comes to sex—you may have experienced sexual abuse as well.

CHEATING

Have you ever known a couple where one person cheated and the other person forgave the other—or at least didn't leave? And you wondered why they would take a cheater back? It's possible that abuse may be involved.

And this can go either way—the abuser may cheat, or the abused may cheat. Not all cheaters are abusers (and vice versa). My experience, however, was that my ex cheated on me—twice.

Because abusers are so good at manipulation, when they cheat, they can often convince their partners that it won't happen again. I stayed with my ex long after he cheated on two completely separate occasions, seven years apart. The manipulative explanation and apologies that followed were so hypnotizing that I don't even remember what he said to convince me to stay, yet I did—and this wasn't even the main reason I left him years later. I did, however, wish he would cheat on me again so I would have an "easy out"—a solid reason to end the relationship.

I learned later that he never meant those apologies. Toward the end of the relationship, I expressed that I had never gotten over his cheating (probably because, intuitively, I knew his apology wasn't genuine). In response, he expressed blatantly that he did not regret doing it. And he punctuated it by bringing in another layer of abuse regarding my sexual performance. Talking about the guy he cheated on me with, he said, "At least he knew what he was doing."

Manipulation is all about the abuser having control over the abused. After my ex cheated on me, we rented a home from the guy whom my ex cheated on me with. Yep. Again, I can't make this shit up. For two full years, I felt uncomfortable in the house where I lived—which, I realize now, essentially mirrors my experience in the entire relationship: uncomfortable in my own home.

By the way, I'm not saying cheating has to be a deal-breaker for all couples, though I do believe it would be in most situations if the non-cheater loves and respects themselves. I also believe that a cheater cheats because of an underlying unhappiness, either with the relationship or with themselves—or both. (This often explains why an abused person cheats.) I'm also not saying that cheating happens in every abusive relationship—again, just an extreme example. But one way or another, cheating is a sign that there's something in the relationship that needs to be addressed.

HOLY COMPLEX TRAUMA, BATMAN

Things weren't good, but they weren't always terrible. I had many moments of crying, begging for peace and happiness, and even hoping for my own demise. (An occasional suicidal thought would enter my mind, but more often it was just wishing to be taken out of this life without my actively doing so—asking God to let me die in my sleep.)

These were not an everyday occurrence, but what I did experience every day was dreading being in the same room with him—or getting a call or text from him when we were apart—because I never knew what to expect. I can still remember the sinking feeling in my stomach when a text message from him would come through on my phone. Which version of him was I going to get in that moment? The unpredictability was unnerving and terrifying.

Abusive relationships can create significant long-term damage. I've learned that I am now in the process of healing from complex post-traumatic stress disorder (C-PTSD), likely largely due to the unpredictable nature of my day-to-day life. I often still get that same sinking feeling in my stomach when I turn the corner around my house to come home because I half-expect him to be waiting for me in the driveway.

In recent months, I've had several nightmares where the two of us are back together—even though my mind knows within the dream that I had gotten out and now need to get back out of the situation. The nightmares often include him chasing me, trapping me, or letting me know I'll be punished for leaving him. After waking from these dreams, because they feel so real, it takes a solid minute or two to realize it was just a dream. But they essentially re-traumatize me for a few moments.

The physical manifestations of trauma recovery vary from person to person. Additional examples include panic attacks, nervous ticks like clenching hands or gritting teeth, crying spells, difficulty breathing, heart palpitations, tremors, high blood pressure, and insomnia.

Meanwhile, from an emotional and mental standpoint, trauma recovery can also cause detachment from loved ones, irritability, anger, and memory loss. In addition to the nightmares (like I described above), we can also experience flashbacks in our waking life. A seemingly random reminder can send us back to a specific event or series of events where we relive the emotional and physical sensations of the trauma.

I'll explain more about the healing journey in a later chapter, but for now, I'll just say that longer and more significant exposure to abuse only creates a more challenging experience in becoming whole again—so it is best to end the abuse as soon as possible.

IGNORING RED FLAGS AND GUT FEELINGS—IT'S WHAT WE DO

Abusive relationships come with all sorts of red flags. Here are some examples from early on in my relationship:

RED FLAG	WHY IT'S A RED FLAG
He repeatedly cheated on an ex-girlfriend with her (male) best friend, and in telling me (and others) about it, he laughed about how "stupid" she was for not realizing what was going on.	A history of cheating increases the likelihood that someone will cheat in a current relationship. His disrespect toward her (both in cheating as well as in describing her ignorance of the matter) reflected how he treats and regards people in general.
He told stories about his "crazy" and abusive ex-boyfriend, including fights that sometimes occurred in public and often dragged on for hours.	His participation in those arguments meant he could very well behave the same way in our relationship. In addition, abusers often say they have "crazy" exes in order to diminish their value and gain sympathy. However, if all their exes are crazy, who's the common denominator here?
He had significant credit card debt that he blamed on his exes.	This shows not only a lack of financial responsibility in racking up debt but also a lack of accepting personal responsibility for his own actions.
We expressed lifelong commitment to each other from the beginning of the relationship (he was twenty-two and I was seventeen).	Abusers tend to rush into commitment at the beginning of relationships. Plus, it takes time to really decide whether another person is a good fit at any age, but we were definitely too young to know whether we would be lifelong partners from the get-go.

All the red flags described above occurred in the first six months of our relationship. At age seventeen, however, I didn't have enough experience to be able to recognize them as warning signs. After the first year of the relationship, I became so accustomed to his behaviors and my uneasy feelings that it all felt normal—even though I can look back now and see all these red flags and the many others that showed up over the years.

On top of the red flags that went unacknowledged, I had gut feelings throughout the relationship that I either didn't know how to recognize or that, intuitively, I did recognize but ignored. (My gut feelings manifest as a literal pang to my stomach, but they can be different for other people. It's something to explore and determine for yourself. You're more intuitive than you may realize.)

> "The moment you begin to wonder if you deserve better, you do."
>
> —PRITESH LAD—

Early in our relationship, I experienced my first gut feeling during a moment of sexual intimacy. Something didn't feel right about us being together. When I analyzed it later, I concluded that my feelings had to do with societal influence since, at the time, gay relationships were not as socially accepted as they are today (and we lived in small towns where being gay was even less accepted).

When he proposed marriage to me, my gut told me to say no. However, he had arranged a surprise proposal in front of a room of fifteen or twenty friends, which pressured me to say yes—and might even have been an intentional move on his part to prevent me from saying no. Still, I'm not sure I would have been brave enough to say no even if it were a private moment. I was convinced we were destined to be together forever, despite my constant angst and unhappiness.

Similar sensations occurred on my wedding day. To me, it's telling that the three gut-wrenching moments I remember most vividly all occurred during times of happiness and enjoyment. In those moments, I was averse to do what was needed because I didn't want to "ruin" the occasion. And like I mistakenly thought during every other positive experience, I hoped and pleaded that the good feelings would continue.

Deep down, I knew better. Things wouldn't remain like that forever (or for very long at all). I felt in my gut what was in my best interest to do. But I hadn't yet built up the courage to act on it.

PROTECTING THE ABUSER

(SAY WHAAAAT?)

One day, a good friend called me in tears and said she needed to scale back on interactions with my ex (which was a nice way of saying cut him out of her life, at least temporarily) after years of abuse toward her. I pleaded with her not to do that and gave excuses for him by saying that he was depressed and going through a tough time. She ultimately agreed not to cut him out because she wanted to maintain a friendship with me—even though maintaining an abusive friendship with him was not in her best interest. I recognize now how unhealthy this approach was. I was only keeping the door open for further abuse toward her, rather than respecting her boundaries and allowing him to experience the consequences of his abusive behavior.

You may have heard the phrase, "Hurt people hurt people." But while a person's own internal issues can *explain* their shitty behavior, they don't *justify* the shitty behavior. News flash: regardless of how many inner demons someone is facing, abusing others is neither appropriate nor acceptable.

Throughout the course of an abusive relationship, we abused people often make excuses for our abusive partners—and defend them not only to other people but also to ourselves. In our minds, we believe that their behavior is understandable or even warranted due to how difficult things are in their lives.

Perhaps even as you read this book, you may be in denial about whether your relationship involves abuse. You don't want to admit your partner is abusive because that is something bad about them, and you would never want to think something bad about them. You may be keeping a blind eye to multiple red flags, all for the simple reason that you need to protect your partner's reputation—even in your own mind.

I often served as an ambassador between my ex and our mutual friends. They would ask me if he was upset with them because he was giving them the silent treatment or treating them especially poorly on the occasion. I would make excuses for him so that they would understand and not hold it against him (or me). Then I would have to placate him in an attempt to keep the peace.

There is a difference between allegiance to your partner versus blind loyalty and overprotection. *We should allow others' behavior to speak for itself and not try to justify or explain it, especially when it harms others.* I also strongly recommend allowing others to hash out their differences without getting involved as the go-between. Their relationship is their business.

HOW BOTH PARTNERS CONTRIBUTE TO AN ABUSIVE RELATIONSHIP

While it's easy to lay all the blame on the abuser, they aren't responsible for everything that goes wrong in an abusive relationship. Both individuals contribute to the dysfunction.

Toxic relationships often involve fighting, screaming, and swearing at each other. However, this is not always the case. Not all people who scream and swear are abusive; some people are just passionate about their beliefs. This intensity can be challenging, though. On the other hand, a toxic relationship may not include fighting at all; instead, there may be passive-aggressive behavior, silent treatment, or suppression of all negative feelings—none of which are healthy.

Meanwhile, there are other unhealthy aspects of abusive relationships that both individuals may take part in—like manipulation, lying, and keeping secrets. For the abused, these are often a measure to protect themselves because being honest and forthright may result in more abuse. In addition, both partners experience mutual resentment toward and obsession about one another.

We all fall somewhere on the spectrum of narcissism, and no one is perfect. I remember occasionally choosing words on purpose that I knew would hurt him the most. This was a defense mechanism when I was provoked, but that doesn't excuse the behavior.

And both of us took part in those screaming matches. There were times in arguments where I experienced a rage so strong that it felt like an out-of-body experience—where I floated up out of my body, looking down at some creature that I didn't recognize. Those moments were scary, and I hope to never experience unhealthy, seemingly uncontrollable anger like that again.

Both individuals in a toxic relationship are also likely out of touch with reality. They deny what is really going on because they can't face the truth; the abuser would never admit to being abusive, and the abused doesn't want to admit that they are being abused because of the potential (unwarranted) shame associated with being a victim. The lack of a grasp on reality may also lead the abused to be enamored with the abuser's potential, rather than with their reality (like I was).

There's a good chance codependency is involved, too, but we'll go into that in the next chapter.

WHY STAY?

Why can't someone in an abusive relationship realize how bad their situation is? And why would someone stay in a relationship like this for so long? As I've recounted my own story, you may be asking yourself, "What took this guy so long to come to his senses? Fifteen years? Holy shit." The reasons are plentiful. Some may make more sense to an outsider than others.

1. **There are good times.** Things are not always bad. I believe that if things in a relationship are never good, most people will know to get out (or work on the relationship if we're talking about one that isn't toxic). In these toxic relationships, however, there are good times, especially in the beginning of the relationship. Perhaps the sex is really good, too—sexual chemistry can often be electric in toxic relationships. As the abused, you latch onto those good times, believe you can go back to them, believe they will continue, or pray that things will get better. (Spoiler alert: they won't.)

2. **The abuse appears gradually over time.** There is a well-known fable describing a frog in boiling water. If a frog is put suddenly into boiling water, it will jump out immediately. On the other hand, if a frog is put in room-temperature water that is slowly brought to a boil, the frog will not realize the danger it's in and will be cooked to death. The same is true for abusive relationships; you may not ever realize the danger you're in because of how gradually the abuse evolves—until it feels normal or it's seemingly too late to get out.

> "When someone shows you who they are, believe them the first time."
>
> —MAYA ANGELOU—

That's why it's so important to pay attention to how you feel throughout the relationship, including moments that make you uncomfortable—even if they seem insignificant at the time.

3. **The manipulation game is strong**—and can cross a wide gamut:
   - If you've been on the receiving end of the tactics abusers use in arguments, you may feel that you own an equal part in why the relationship is failing. You come to believe that there is so much for you to work on, and if you just make all of those changes, then maybe your partner will finally treat you better and love you the way you want to be loved.
   - Your partner will also have you convinced that things will get better. They will be nicer, more respectful, more considerate, and more patient. The relationship is littered with false promises.
   - Your partner will convince you that they are the only one who will "put up with" you and that life without them will be a life alone and miserable.
   - On the flipside, your partner may also go to great lengths to convince you that they can't (or won't) live without you. Pleading, desperate moments can include such phrases as "I don't know what I'd do without you" and "You're the only good thing going on in my life." Your partner may go so far as to threaten suicide if you leave.

4. **You believe you can fix them.** As we'll discuss in the upcoming chapter on codependency, you may feel obligated to stay with your partner because you believe you can fix them (by healing their emotional wounds and making them a better person) or that it's your responsibility to cure their physical, emotional, or mental illness. And along those lines, if you are able to see the darkness of your partner's self-hatred, you may feel you can cure this by loving them harder and longer than desired. What you don't yet realize is that your love for your abusive partner will never be stronger than their need for abuse and control.

5. **You believe it's normal.** If you are inexperienced with relationships, you may believe that what is happening is normal and to be expected. My relationship with my ex was the only adult relationship I had ever experienced. And I had always heard that "relationships are hard work," so I thought I had to just suck it up and deal with it. Relationships do take work and effort to maintain, but the work doesn't need to be painful—definitely not to the level that many abused people experience.

6. **Abuse is all you know.** Regardless of whether you have been in other relationships, it's possible to be conditioned to believe that abuse is a normal part of a romantic relationship because it's all you know. Many individuals in this situation may have had parents who abused each other or their children. *Growing up in a toxic environment can cause you to believe this is normal—and even if you recognize that it's not normal, a lack of healing from these traumatic experiences can attract the same types of relationships in adulthood.* And again, the relationship likely doesn't start out as abusive—if the abuse appears slowly over time, it may not be evident until it's seemingly past the point of no return.

7. **You are financially dependent.** As described in the earlier section on financial abuse, targets can be (or become) financially dependent on their partners, which makes them feel unable to live on their own. This can be a big one; in fact, it may be the *only* reason some people stay in an abusive relationship.

8. **You don't want to break up the family.** You may have kids together and not want to disrupt the current state. While, thankfully, this never applied to me, I would assert here an important lesson: when we do the most loving thing for ourselves,

we're doing the most loving thing for those around us as well. I've included more on this in the next chapter, but for now, think about the example this sets for the kids to see their parents stay together out of obligation when they are clearly unhappy. This may become ingrained in their minds as a model for relationships, which could lead to the same behaviors and attract the same relationship dynamics in their adulthood. Is that what you want?

9. **You made a commitment.** Another factor is having made a commitment, especially after having signed that marriage license. Because divorce still has somewhat of a stigma associated with it, you may feel resistance to the idea, often because it has a connotation of failure. But people change—the person we meet is often not the same person five, ten, or thirty years later—so it's a question of whether that new, current version of your partner is still a good fit for you. Before giving up, I think it's important to honor a commitment and work on the relationship, either with each other or through professional guidance. However, for continuing the relationship to make sense, both partners simultaneously have to (1) be willing to put in the effort; (2) value the relationship enough; and (3) feel safe, comfortable, and loved even during times of challenge and growth. Otherwise, personal happiness should take precedence over commitment to a relationship that is no longer working or that no longer feels right.

10. **You've been together for so long.** As in any failing relationship, there can be the "sunk cost fallacy,"[3] a term from behavioral economics that refers to a human's continuation of a behavior or endeavor as a result of previously invested time, money, or effort. In other words, a couple may stay together simply because they have been together for so long.

> "Don't cling to a mistake just because you spent a lot of time making it."
>
> —UNKNOWN—

---

3. "Sunk Cost Fallacy," BehavioralEconomics.com, accessed February 28, 2021, https://www.behavioraleconomics.com/resources/mini-encyclopedia-of-be/sunk-cost-fallacy.

It's like forcing yourself to finish the food or drink in front of you (when you're already miserable) just to "get your money's worth" or because you know it won't be good the next day. You may not want to "throw away" all those years of memories, even if things in the present are a complete train wreck. This is understandable. This is human. However, this is also bullshit. It's called a *fallacy* for a reason—it lacks sound logic. The underlying reasons are usually fear of the unknown and a lack of individual identity outside of the relationship.

11. **The abuser denies you from getting help.** Therapy ultimately put me on the path to realize this relationship was no longer working—but because of the abuse layer in the relationship, I felt like I could not seek outside help until I had finally reached my rock bottom. Until then, he told me that all of our relationship issues needed to remain between the two of us with no discussion of them outside the relationship—and I obeyed. When he found out I had one isolated therapy session with a counselor a few years prior to the end of our relationship, he was extremely upset. He told me he felt betrayed that I didn't tell him because keeping secrets from him was not acceptable. While I agree secrets are not healthy, I believe the *real* reason he was upset was that I was seeking help for my own betterment and potentially speaking poorly about him to someone else. (*Psst*, that's totally what I did.)

Perhaps this is obvious, but since it wasn't obvious to me, I'll say it again—there are about five dozen red flags associated with a partner who discourages you from seeking therapy. Any healthy relationship involves two people who only want the best for each other, and I believe therapy can benefit everyone—even those who are doing really well. So there is no reason to discourage therapy unless there are ulterior motives, none of which I would imagine are well-intentioned. (Note: an argument of "we can't afford it" is likely covering up other motives. If it's important to you, you can find a way to make it work financially—and your partner should be supportive of this.)

Of course, looking back, I see now that there were all sorts of reasons to leave that relationship—but at the time, many of the counteractive reasons I listed above ultimately prevented me from getting out permanently.

We "broke up" temporarily a couple of times (yet still lived together!) and tried an open relationship at one point, during which times I thrived and was the happiest and freest I had ever felt. Then when we got back together and things returned to "normal," I would be unhappy again. Yet I stayed with him for another decade. Oh, the things I could scream at that younger version of myself! But at the time, I just didn't see what is obvious to me now.

Love is not blind, but love through emotional abuse is blinding. Healthy relationships help make us more certain about ourselves and our choices. On the contrary, emotional abuse kills our ability to make decisions and trust our own instincts. We question everything our minds and hearts tell us, even when it's obvious that we are unhappy.

THEY WON'T CHANGE, SO GET THE HELL OUT

"Is there hope my partner will change?" For abused people (including myself), this is the million-dollar question.

For abusers who do not fall into the category of a narcissist, sociopath, or psychopath, there may be hope—but it will require significant work and willingness from the abuser to change.

As to whether a narcissist, sociopath, or psychopath can change, the realistic answer is no. While, theoretically, anyone can change their behavior and way of thinking with the help of professionals, the first step in any life change is admitting there is a problem—which will never happen for these individuals because, by nature, they do not and will never believe anything is wrong with them.

You might be thinking, "What about couples counseling?" Also no. Individual counseling for yourself, absolutely—make that appointment now. But again, there will not be any change in the behavior of a narcissist, sociopath, or psychopath. And because these individuals are masters of manipulation, they can actually convince therapists to be on their side (unless the therapist has experience working with these individuals and can recognize them for who they truly are). The therapist might fall victim to their spell, whether the things the abuser shares or promises during those sessions are truthful or not.

You can navigate these types of relationships with the help of individual therapy, reading, and online support groups. But ultimately, *the only way for your life to dramatically improve is to leave and cut off all contact with your abuser.* Without cutting off contact, you run the risk of being looped back into yet another cycle of empty promises that they will change and begin treating you better. But sooner or later, the patterns will continue—only this time, it may be even worse, a punishment for leaving.

For some, cutting off contact is not an option due to shared custody of children or the need for financial support. My heart goes out to these individuals. While I was not in that situation, I do have some suggestions:

1. Do your best to get out and limit contact with them as much as possible.
2. Equally important: get your ass into therapy!
3. The Facebook group "Living with Narcissist Emotional Abuse" provides support for targets and survivors of these relationships and may be able to provide additional guidance. I believe there are other groups like this as well, but I don't have personal experience with them to be able to provide a recommendation.
4. The other resources at the back of this book may also be helpful.

Without the constraints of kids or finances, the best solution for you is to run and never look back. Ending my toxic relationship was one of the best decisions I've ever made, and I'll go into more detail on that in the next chapter.

Throughout the remainder of this book, I'll describe some aspects of my own healing journey. But as far as the topic of abuse and what can be done if you're in an abusive relationship, the first steps are to get out and get help—not necessarily in that order.

IN CLOSING

For the vast majority of my relationship, I knew I was unhappy but didn't fully understand why. I knew there were problems that needed fixing, but I didn't know how to fix them. When I would engage in discussions with my ex about our relationship and how we could and should make it better, it would always lead to a fight. Or more often, it was the reverse—a fight would lead to me trying to discuss these opportunities for improvement, which would only lead to more fighting. And, my word, were those fights emotionally exhausting.

Healthy relationships don't involve fighting. Disagreements? Absolutely. Hurt feelings? Maybe. But the "knock-down, drag-out" fights of screaming at each other, calling each other names, sobbing because of how one partner treats the other, or getting physical with each other are all characteristics of an unhealthy relationship. If tensions run so high that disagreements escalate to this level of drama, it's time to seek help— for yourself individually, for you as a couple, or both (unless your partner is a narcissist, sociopath, or psychopath—in which case, only individual therapy will be beneficial).

Trust me—speaking from experience, I can say with confidence that *a life full of constant build up and release of toxic tension is not sustainable.* We stick around because we believe things will get better. How many not-so-merry-go-rounds of that cycle of abuse will it take before you finally decide it's not for you and jump the hell off?

On the other hand, in the early parts of these relationships, we may not have been through enough of those cycles to recognize our unhappiness yet. That's why I'm here: to help you recognize the warning signs as early on as possible. If any aspects of my abuse remind you of your current relationship(s), it's important to take the first step of being aware of this and observing how things develop. Remember that our level of denial can be significant because we don't want to admit that we're "one of those people" trapped in the types of situations I've described here. There's no shame in it—it happens to the best of us (like yours truly).

In fact, that is precisely where it usually happens. Because abusers are full of hate and lack loving energy, they latch on to the most caring, loving, empathic people because they have the highest amount of loving energy for the abusers to try and absorb. Abusers like the challenge of a "project" like us because it takes time and meticulous strategy to get what they want, which feels like a great accomplishment to them when they do achieve it. And if they do it correctly, they can manage to feed on a "supply" that will last for years, if not a lifetime.

I believe that self-worth (the value we give ourselves) is the key to overcoming abuse. We allow other people to treat us however we feel we deserve. We won't tolerate anything beyond that threshold. Once I began taking care of myself and recognizing my worth, my threshold of what I would tolerate became lower, which allowed me to quickly conclude that I could not tolerate my ex's treatment of me any longer.

By that point, I understood that ending the relationship was not "giving up"—I had done all I could to save the relationship. Instead, leaving him was the most loving thing I could do for both of us.

I recognize now what abuse taught me about happiness. When I share these experiences with people, they often say, "Oh, I'm so sorry you went through that." While I understand where that sentiment comes from, I usually respond by expressing my gratitude for the experience. The relationship provided contrast to show me what I did *not* want to feel or experience. It allowed me to learn what I *did* want to experience once I was able to move on. Then I could know what the real deal is when it would come along.

—REFLECTION—

What relationships in your life are abusive? What aspects of them are abusive? What can you do to change the dynamic of these relationships?

ADDICTION & CODEPENDENCY

Everyone wants to be happy, but some people seek happiness from the wrong places. If we aren't happy with ourselves or with our other relationships, we may look to fill that gap in unhealthy ways.

There are many different kinds of addiction—both chemical (drugs and alcohol) and behavioral (e.g., relationships, sex, shopping, workaholism). People with addictive personalities tend to develop more than one addiction, although there is usually one that gets the ball rolling (for example, alcoholism leading to sex addiction).

Codependency, also known as "relationship addiction," describes relationships that are one-sided, emotionally destructive, or abusive. They prevent either individual from having a healthy, mutually satisfying experience with the other. Codependency often develops in relationships that involve chemical addiction, abuse, and physical or mental illness. In fact, codependency was originally a term that was specifically reserved for people in relationships with addicts.[4]

Because of this relationship between codependency and chemical addiction—and because chemical addiction feeds codependency and vice versa—the lines are often blurred as to where one ends and another begins. You'll notice this as I go into detail about my experience with both in my relationship.

---

4. "Co-Dependency," Mental Health America, accessed February 22, 2021, https://www.mhanational.org/issues/co-dependency.

We'll also discuss the impact that addiction has on the ultimate fate of relationships. While it is possible for a relationship to survive addiction, it will require having a good handle on that addiction for both people to feel safe with one another. We'll talk a bit regarding how to go about this.

Whether the relationship continues or ends, however, addiction presents many challenges for both individuals. Ultimately, deciding the next steps requires a hard look at both the relationship and ourselves.

CHEMICAL ADDICTION

My experience with chemical addiction was exposure to the effects of ongoing overuse of alcohol, but what I'm about to share relates to the use of other chemical substances as well. And there are more layers to my story than "just" alcohol.

My ex and I both drank too much. We met when I was seventeen and he was twenty-two, and I left him fifteen years later. Alcohol was a key part of our lives for that entire time.

For many years, I don't believe I went a day without having at least one alcoholic beverage. This was primarily an unhealthy coping mechanism for dealing with a stressful job and relationship. In addition, given the abusive nature of our relationship, I also felt peer pressure to drink. Not drinking would be met with derision, ridicule, and a guilt trip; thus, for my own safety, well-being, and sanity, I drank.

But I still made those unhealthy choices for myself, and I own that. However, it wasn't just the alcohol—I made poor choices while drinking, too. I can't tell you how many times I drove under the influence—on a few occasions, heavily under the influence. I am damn lucky I didn't hurt myself—or anyone else.

Fortunately, I came to my senses. I began to realize all the long-term effects this excessive drinking was having on my mind and body—poor sleep, escalated emotions and reactions, worsened depression, and memory loss. That last one was what really made me wake up. One area of success for me was in my career, and I was forgetting details of projects and conversations that I would normally be on top of with no problem. I couldn't let that continue—I couldn't let my performance falter in one of the only places in my life where things were actually going well.

For those reasons, I knew I had to cut back significantly, and I did. I continued to drink every day, but it was down to one or two low-alcohol beverages most days. At this point, my top two reasons for drinking flipped their order—the primary one became peer pressure from my ex, followed by an unhealthy coping mechanism for stress.

Medically speaking, I don't believe I was ever considered an alcoholic, but I definitely abused alcohol. My unhealthy dependence and addiction were to something besides booze. (Ooh, foreshadowing!)

My ex, on the other hand, had a severe addiction to alcohol—one that nearly killed him. He had unexplained health issues related to seizures and cognition for more than a decade, and these issues all came to a head in events that I recognize now as my rock bottom.

For years, his health was unsteady (to say the least), and I viewed myself as his full-time caretaker. I arranged all of his doctor appointments, handled everything related to his health insurance, took copious notes throughout the process, and soul-searched with various family and friends to brainstorm ideas in the hope of finding answers.

The most draining aspect of caretaking, however, had to do with essentially acting as a nurse during his various episodes of any combination of dizziness, weakness, unsteadiness, nausea, confusion, disorientation, memory loss, severe headaches, body aches, muscle pain, chest pain, seeing visions, impaired breathing, and mini-seizures. Imagine watching your partner suffer through these ailments on a regular basis without having any clue as to what to do, why it was happening, or how to make things better.

It eventually became a nightly occurrence where I would have to help him to bed at an early hour and then make sure he got to sleep, which could take anywhere from a few minutes to a few hours. I felt like a parent with a newborn or sick child, not a spouse.

In our wedding vows, we agreed to take each other in sickness and in health, and I was willing to do that. My resentments and frustrations here had to do with the emotional abuse that layered on top of the health issues. The things he shouted and spewed at me while I tried to do what was best for him did not make this a task that I enjoyed or even tolerated doing at times. Telling me I was a terrible caretaker, for example, was not good motivation to continue caretaking.

It didn't take long to recognize that the more he drank, the worse his symptoms became. Thus, I became frustrated when I would bring this to his attention and he would continue to drink just as much. He would either dismiss my concerns as being too dramatic or manipulate me by promising to cut back on drinking, only to be back to the same or even a larger amount of alcohol the next day.

He usually had no memory of his episodes, but I sure did. And this took a toll on me emotionally, mentally, and physically. I resented him for not taking measures to improve his health—if not for his own benefit, then for the sake of my sanity.

Given those frustrations and the fact that he was essentially out of his mind during these episodes, I would inevitably leave him many nights to fall asleep on his own. Why witness something so heartbreaking and terrifying—and feel so helpless and borderline insane—if I didn't have to? But I would sit downstairs and try to escape reality, all the while hearing his moans of pain, which layered on a level of guilt that I wasn't doing more to help.

To add insult to injury, after years of his convincing me that all our problems had to remain between us, I didn't feel like I could confide in anyone with much of any detail, and I didn't want to embarrass or speak poorly of him. Thus, I felt completely alone in having to face these challenges.

I also resented him for how many plans with friends and family we had to cancel because he "wasn't feeling well," when again I felt like he could improve things if he would just cut back on the booze.

I wanted to figure out the source of his health problems so that our lives could return to "normal." (Not exactly sure what "normal" would have looked like, either—but that's beside the point.) However, no medical tests showed conclusive results. Of course, he was low-balling his alcohol intake at each of these visits. This was critical information the doctors would have needed to apply an appropriate and clear diagnosis. Alcohol use impacts the effectiveness of seizure medication; increases the likelihood of seizure activity; and endangers one's life when combined with drugs like Xanax, which he was also taking.

I felt confused, hopeless, desperate, tired, empty, and alone. My life was a mess, and I so badly wanted and needed a break. Sometimes I cried; sometimes I just sat emotionless and stone-faced. I was tired. Drained.

Little did I know that, after fourteen challenging years together—most of which included these health issues—things were about to get significantly worse. (Buckle up.)

Eventually, these health issues resulted in the loss of his job, and the ten months that followed brought significant challenges that ultimately played a major role in our relationship ending. His condition worsened significantly—not only the substance abuse but also his depression and anxiety. He became more and more of a zombie. Even though he was home all day, his productivity around the house was practically non-existent—it would be a good day if he emptied the dishwasher.

I urged him to seek therapy, which he did for a few months and asked me to join him in the sessions. But there was no change. He refused to try any of the homework assignments his therapist gave him. He also low-balled his alcohol intake with her, so she did not have the full picture of what was going on. She diagnosed him with severe clinical depression and recommended that he obtain an anti-depressant from his physician.

This next step only made everything worse. His physician not only prescribed an anti-depressant but also myriad other new drugs and an increase to existing prescriptions. At age thirty-six, my ex was on nine daily prescriptions—oh, and still drinking, by the way.

His body had a severe reaction to get these various poisons out of his system. For a week or two, the man couldn't walk on his own. I had to help him to and from the bathroom. I still remember his screams of pain and complete confusion as to what was going on. I also remember wondering how the hell we had gotten to that point. It didn't seem like things could get any worse. I kept thinking:

I can't do this.

I can't live like this.

I just want out.

I insisted on a few different occasions that we go to the hospital, but he refused. And I allowed his refusal to dictate what we would do (or rather, not do)—even though it felt to me like his life was in danger.

Nonetheless, I knew something had to change. Now completely distrustful of our physician, I took the liberty on my own of weaning him off all the new medications so that we could start from square one.

He returned to a seemingly normal state, though I didn't realize just how much damage had been done to his body and mind by this point. He continued to drink every night, and I learned later that he started to drink hard alcohol in the mornings as well, which he hid from me. And over the course of the next few months, he attended a couple of major multi-day out-of-town events, neither of which he later could remember happening at all.

Meanwhile, the severity of his alcohol addiction also began to rope other addictive behaviors into his life (our lives), namely shopping and sex. These were never diagnosed per se, but the obsession with these (sex in particular) became just as all-consuming as his focus on alcohol. Expanding into other addictive behaviors is common among addicts.

The continued substance abuse finally led to a night of three grand mal seizures (the most violent type of seizures with limbs thrashing and mouth foaming). I called 911, and paramedics came to the house to take him to the emergency room. He was admitted to the ICU for a full week.

His diagnosis was unclear for the first two days—again because he was not forthright about his alcohol intake.

However, once he began having hallucinations, the doctors immediately attributed his symptoms to alcohol withdrawal and began the detoxification process from both alcohol and Xanax—a combination, I was later told, is one of the most lethal chemical combinations to detox from. The medical team had to follow a precise detox protocol of dosage and frequency, or he easily could have died.

The clinicians also told me that had I not called 911 that night, there was a real possibility he could have died. His body was so dependent on alcohol that it couldn't go *eight hours* without it and not go into shock. On the spectrum of alcoholism severity, my ex was just one step short of death. The seizures were his body's way of crying out for help.

That night of witnessing the three grand mal seizures and the following week of alcohol withdrawal in the ICU were an experience I would not wish on my worst enemy. Throughout most of that week, my heart was in my throat; otherwise, my entire body was mostly numb. I was in shock.

Alcohol withdrawal involves hallucinations, paranoia, irritability beyond belief, and a total loss of self. There were moments I was convinced that a demon was trapped inside him. His anger escalated to levels I had never seen before (which is really saying something, trust me). One day, he ripped out the IV needles from his arms out of frustration toward me. The next day, in the heat of another argument, I was convinced by his shakiness and the wideness of his eyes that he was about to hit me. That was the moment I realized I had to let go and leave his side. His well-being was out of my hands, and my presence was only making things worse for both of us.

At the end of that horrific week, when it was obvious that he did not recognize the severity of his condition, I arranged an intervention with his family in which I was clear that I did not plan to stick around if he did not agree to get professional help. He reluctantly, begrudgingly agreed to check himself into inpatient alcohol rehabilitation. His decision gave me hope that we were headed in the right direction.

That week, between the seizures and the experience in the ICU, was a total nightmare and brought my rock bottom. As I witnessed my husband's body, mind, and spirit deteriorate right in front of me, I felt complete loss of control—no knowledge of what to do next. I had seen the deterioration increasing over the years leading up to that week, but they had all finally reached their peak.

This may surprise you, but I am grateful for everything that led up to this moment, including the experience of my rock bottom. From that point on, things continued to get better for me. I gained clarity and perspective about myself, him, and our relationship that I had been blind to seeing for so long. I finally began to seek help.

CODEPENDENCY: THE RELATIONSHIP ADDICTION

Less than a week later, I had my first therapy session. One of the most memorable moments from that meeting was when my therapist pointed out that, just like my ex was addicted to alcohol, I was addicted to him. I wasn't clear what that meant at the time, but I soon learned and agreed with the truth of it. And for those of you still wondering why the hell I stayed in that relationship for so long, there's your answer—well, one of the reasons, at least.

Through both therapy and Al-Anon meetings, I began to learn about codependency. (Al-Anon is similar to Alcoholics Anonymous but exists for the benefit of the loved ones of alcoholics.)

Let's take a brief pause from the story of the last few months of my relationship so I can share what I learned about relationship addiction and how those lessons ultimately factored into my decision to end my marriage.

Although it was (and still is) difficult to admit, my codependency meant that my behavior was making the situation worse for both of us. I enabled his addiction and his abusive treatment of me. Lack of boundaries meant lack of clarity as to where he stopped and where I began—enmeshment with each other's identity, behavior, emotions, and well-being.

What do I mean by boundaries? These are guidelines or limits that a person creates to identify and communicate reasonable, safe, and permissible ways for other people to behave toward them—and how they will respond when someone pushes those limits. Boundaries also distinguish one person's responsibility from another person's responsibility to act, think, and feel for themselves.

It's important to note that not all codependent relationships are as abusive or volatile as what I described in the previous chapter. They are certainly not healthy for either individual, but the impact can be more subtle. Both chemical addicts and codependents can be pleasant and agreeable. (After all, I'm a recovering codependent, and I've always had a winning personality!)

52

It was and continues to be difficult to own my part in how unhealthy this relationship was. It has always been easier to lay all the blame on him for being the one who was emotionally abusive and drank too much—and don't get me wrong, those behaviors created all sorts of challenges for us and traumatized me. However, I definitely played a role in contributing toward our dysfunction.

The key roles of a codependent relationship can be illustrated with the diagram below, known as the Drama Triangle:

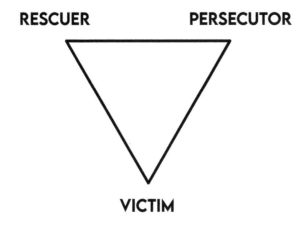

It's called the Drama Triangle for a reason—interactions in codependent relationships can be intensely dramatic. However, drama does not equate to love, no matter how much love either individual feels for the other. And drama like this most definitely is not healthy.

Each individual in a codependent relationship often exhibits all three of these personas at various times, and my relationship was no exception to this rule. I was primarily a rescuer but assumed the other roles at times as well.

My coming to his rescue didn't serve either of us. Because I perceived him as a victim who needed to be saved, I would often fight his battles for him—whether it was defending his inappropriate behavior with our friends and family, managing his health, enabling his drinking, or even calling in sick to work on his behalf. Granted, he often asked me to do these things (or demanded that I do them), but the fact that I complied only opened the door for the behavior to continue in the future.

His lack of gratitude for everything I did for him frustrated me, which shifted me into the role of a persecutor. I would think things like, "How dare he not acknowledge the time and effort I'm putting into making his life better?" and "Will he ever get his shit together and pull his own weight?" Rarely did I voice these feelings, though, because enabling took precedence as part of my primary role as a rescuer.

And because the relationship involved abuse, I often found myself in the victim role with him as the persecutor. I would then rely on him to rescue me from those feelings of victimhood—instead of doing what I needed to do to take care of myself—so that I could shift back to my role as the rescuer. The pattern would then continue in no particular order.

Rescuers like myself—or "people pleasers"—need to be needed. I would often take on too much for my own good—saying yes when I wanted or needed to say no. Again, boundaries were blurry. My rescuing and people-pleasing tended to just apply to the relationship with my ex and not others, though there were some exceptions. Many rescuers struggle with more than one relationship.

When I look back at old emails between us, I can see some glimmers that I realized how unhealthy my rescuing was. Over the years, I sent him lists of neurologists and counselors for him to make an appointment—and then six to twelve months later, I'd send another list because he hadn't done anything and the problems had continued or gotten worse. I was attempting to put the ball in his court—to encourage him to take care of his own health because I knew that should be his job, not mine. But because these attempts failed, I would resort to taking care of things myself.

I felt I was responsible for his livelihood and even his thoughts, feelings, and behavior—and conversely, I allowed him to determine how I should feel, act, behave, and think. I blamed him for my behavior (whether or not I voiced this to him) and blamed myself for his behavior.

A power shift occurred approximately five years into our relationship. Until that point, I felt I could not live without him. Then two major betrayals occurred—he stole that $13,000 from the nonprofit and later cheated on me for the second time. I decided to stay with him after both incidents because I began to feel instead that *he* could not live without *me*, which led me to feel obligated to stay with him regardless of how unhappy

I was. It's possible it was always the case that he could not live without me, even since the beginning, and I just didn't see it. Either way, neither of these scenarios is healthy. *The two partners in a relationship should be equals; there shouldn't be a hierarchy.*

My happiness was contingent on his being happy. There's that enmeshment again. I thought if I could help him along and arrange things in his life to make him happy, then I could be happy, too. I had no thought of trying to make myself happy first—he was always priority number one. This prioritization may surprise you, given what I just said about the hierarchy, but having the upper hand is exactly where my role as a rescuer originated.

Speaking of which, self-care was also nonexistent in my life. The concept of it seemed selfish to me as I had always learned to put others' needs before mine. Another major lesson I had to learn as part of my therapy was the important difference between *selfish* and *self-loving*. Again, when we do the most loving thing for ourselves, we, in turn, give everyone around us exactly what they need, too. (I'll go more into the idea of self-love later.)

Just as I always put his needs before mine, I was always more concerned about protecting him than I was about protecting myself and more worried about his feelings than my own. I knew that any negative feelings or unhappiness he felt would ultimately impact me—in other words, my feelings were dependent on his.

That's also why I often didn't express opinions unless I agreed with him. I didn't feel like I was allowed to have an opinion that differed from his. He hated how often I said, "I don't care" or "Whatever you want," but I didn't feel I had a choice. Doing whatever he wanted was the path of least resistance. The only way I could be happy was if he was happy.

I also had a strong need to control things whenever I possibly could— probably because I had lost my ability to control most of my unpredictable everyday life. I would sit and ruminate about all possible future scenarios so that I could plan how I would react to and handle them. More often than not, even when one of my predictions would come true (which was uncommon), I wouldn't be able to control my own reaction, and things would not go according to my plan. I was plagued by fear and anxiety over my inability to control situations or have any sort of power over my own life. And I wasted so much time worrying about the future.

Codependency has a number of negative impacts, including (but not limited to) resentment, stress, exhaustion, loss of identity, emotional repression and numbness, physical illness, weight loss or weight gain, guilt, fear, sexual dissociation, chemical addiction, lack of fulfillment, and loss of control. I experienced all of these.

While my ex and I each had different individual experiences in our relationship, there were several common aspects to our experience, which I've listed below. In these instances, we weren't so different after all.

(Note: I've included here my perception of what my ex experienced. As a narcissist, he would often lie to me and manipulate me as to how he felt, so I can't say with 100 percent certainty that these were his experiences. But this is what I either perceived at the time or came to understand and believe—either through my own experiences or through learning things in therapy, Al-Anon, research, and education.)

1. Obviously, we were both there for all of our fights. The amount of anger, interruption, and screaming was not healthy by any standards. And alcohol only made things worse. Emotions would trigger the perceived need to drink, followed by heightened emotions, followed by more drinking, and so on.

2. Both of us suffered from anxiety. The tension and unpredictability of any given situation left me constantly feeling on edge. The slightest bit of stress could set either of us off and provoke any variety of reactions.

3. Both of us experienced depression and felt alone. For him, I believe it came from a complete lack of self-worth and self-love. I believe my depression was situational instead of clinical (which I'll explain in the next chapter). My energy, identity, and sense of life had all been drained out of me. And alcohol further exacerbated both of our experiences with depression.

4. Both of us were obsessed with alcohol but in different ways—he obsessed about drinking it; I obsessed about his drinking it. And prior to my realizing he was an alcoholic, we both always needed to make sure that outings could include alcohol so that he would enjoy himself.

5. Both of us felt trapped with no way out of our unhappiness.

6. Both of us were so unhappy that we expressed wanting to die. It's not clear to me whether he ever meant it when he said he was considering suicide, but it certainly came up. And I fantasized somewhat regularly about dying. I thought things would be so much easier if I weren't here.

7. Our issues, both individual and in the relationship, were debilitating and all-consuming. There was such a confusing mix of hatred and love (or at least what I thought was love) toward ourselves and each other all the time.

Without these commonalities, it may seem like the abuser/addict and the target/codependent are two totally different roles in the relationship. But while there are key differences, there are also some important similarities that contribute to the dysfunction.

My addiction has been a difficult one from which to recover. Months after leaving him, I found myself still wanting to "take a hit" of the drama to which I had grown so accustomed. My life had become somewhat boring without it! Gradually, though, I've learned how much more satisfying peacefulness is. But I'm still a work in progress.

ENDING MY RELATIONSHIP

So, back to my story. Where were we? My ex had checked into inpatient alcoholic rehabilitation just one day before my first therapy session. Following my rock bottom and introduction to codependency, approximately three months passed before I left my ex. Let's discuss the events from that three-month period.

He spent too short a time in rehab (just one week) and came home a "dry drunk." This refers to someone whose refraining from alcohol is so new that they still grapple with the emotional and psychological triggers that may have fueled the addiction to begin with. Thus, alcohol continues to have a strong hold on the mind. The addict's mind perceives the substance to be the cure for its problems. The chemical need for alcohol (even in a situation like this, where he had gone through a full detoxification process) causes the individual to lash out at their loved ones.

In an already abusive relationship, you can imagine what kind of experience this was. His resentment toward me was palpable. He viewed me as the barrier that kept him from what he needed and made sure to let me know this through how he treated me.

I set boundaries with him for possibly the first time and told him that I expected him to continue getting treatment and professional help and to not drink. When the boundaries were received with anger and complete disregard, I could see his level of disrespect for me (and himself), as well as where his priorities lay.

I promised myself and everyone close to us that I would stick with him through one relapse—and beyond that, he would need to get help, or I would leave. I had learned that most addicts experience at least one relapse before deciding for themselves that they need to get help, so I thought maybe that would be the case for him—all the while remaining quite concerned about what relapse would look like since the first round almost killed him.

Lo and behold, without ongoing professional help, he relapsed within a few weeks. He started out "slow" with low-alcohol-content beverages, but it wasn't long before he was back to drinking on a daily basis again, which I had told him was unacceptable. But just because I was learning to set boundaries didn't mean he took them seriously or respectfully.

And then there was the constant lying. There's a well-known joke that asks, "How do you know an addict is lying?" The answer: "His lips are moving." It's funny because it's true. Sometimes the lies were obvious—other times not. But either way, it was truly mind-boggling because it often seemed even *he* believed his own lies.

The unpredictability of the things he would say and do during that time was utterly baffling. I'll give you an example. Because he had found more energy and motivation, he had begun searching for jobs again. I'll never forget our conversation when he suggested to me, with complete sincerity and conviction, how great of an idea it would be for him to pursue a career in bartending. Again, I can't make this shit up.

The drinking quickly escalated to a point that I packed a bag and let him know I would be staying elsewhere for a while to think things through. In that conversation, he threatened suicide if I were to leave. I believed his emotional pleas, feared what might happen if I sought the needed time alone to think, and agreed to stay—with the stipulation that he seek help.

He agreed to seek counseling in the form of traditional talk therapy. I later learned that this would likely not have done him any good unless it had led him to complete his rehabilitation program. Talk therapy by itself will only be beneficial to someone whose system has recovered from chemical dependency. Even so, I thought his agreement to this was a step in the right direction.

I realized later that both the suicide threat and his agreement to get help were yet additional forms of manipulation. Both convinced me to stay, and he didn't care how extreme the measures were. Whatever it took.

Therapy was another instance when he said one thing but meant another. One day he would express wanting therapy for himself; the next day, he would resent my attendance of individual therapy and Al-Anon meetings (what he referred to as my "cult"). Fortunately, by this point, I had prioritized seeking help for my own benefit over whatever he felt about it. He knew his only way of keeping me around was for me not to grow, learn, and expand. He knew that with objective and supportive input, I would soon realize how toxic our relationship was and that I deserved better than he treated me. He could see the writing on the wall.

Meanwhile, I became aware for the first time what a narcissist was and what others experienced in toxic, emotionally abusive relationships. Until that point, I thought my experience was unique and that no one else would understand. I quickly found and joined that Facebook support group (Living with Narcissist Emotional Abuse), for whom I am eternally grateful.

If I hadn't hit rock bottom, I may have never discovered all of this helpful information. I might still be stuck in year seventeen of that relationship as I type this. That experience in the ICU was a blessing in disguise that allowed my mind to reset and gain new perspective about my life and our relationship.

I learned through that process that narcissists have zero ability to change who they are because that would require admitting fault or that something is wrong with them. By connecting the dots, I realized that even if he were to eventually get sober (which was unlikely), the emotional abuse would continue—and I wasn't about to stick around for more of that.

In the midst of finding a divorce attorney and even beginning the process of filling out paperwork, I was still only about 95 percent sure that I would leave him. But because I knew how unlikely it was for a miracle to happen, I arranged numerous logistics so that things would be ready to go whenever I decided to pull the trigger. I opened my own bank account, made a list of items to take with me, and notified just one personal friend about my plan. Then, in a matter of a couple of weeks, I made my decision.

The defining moment was less than climactic and really just more of the same. During yet another hour-long debate about whether he should be drinking or not, I thought to myself, "Why am I fighting him on this? I'm done. I'm just done." And that was that. I didn't let on as to my decision, but I told him in that moment to do whatever he wanted as far as booze. And for the next two weeks that we were together, he drank every day. Left to his own devices, he made it clear what his priority was. Meanwhile, I looked for my opportunity to get the hell out, which was challenging because he was always home with me.

Because of the unpredictable nature of his behavior, and the previous suicide threat, I concluded with the help of the online support group and my therapist that my only choice was to leave him with absolutely no con-tact between us to follow. Since that day, we have had no direct contact. This was the only way to ensure my own safety and the ability to move on in a healthy manner. And while it was an incredibly difficult, stressful, and painful decision, it is one of the best decisions I've ever made.

The day I left him was an emotional rollercoaster, to say the least. He finally left the house, and I knew he would be gone for at least a couple of hours. This was my opportunity. As I scrambled to pack, I remember pausing to think, "Is this really happening right now? Is this really my life?" I had made a thorough, lengthy list of items to pack in prepara-tion for that day, but it was still a blur and a bit of a panic to actually make it happen. I was simultaneously anxiety-ridden (shaking and short of breath) while also feeling numb.

Fortunately, I was able to leave my house and head immediately toward a previously scheduled appointment with my therapist—talk about good timing. There, I broke down crying because I was finally able to sit down and relax, away from the chaos. Given his previous threats, I was consumed with worry that he would physically harm himself, or worse—and if he did, it would be my fault because I left. My therapist reminded me that he was already killing himself through the self-destructive behavior he had chosen to continue—he was "just taking the slow route."

She also reminded me that leaving him was, in fact, the most loving thing I could do for him because it was the only way he would ever get better. Continuing in that relationship would have only further enabled his inappropriate behavior toward me and his own self-destruction.

> "I didn't leave because I stopped loving you. I left because the longer I stayed, the less I loved myself."
>
> —RUPI KAUR—

The "no contact rule" is an important one to stick to for maximum efficiency when it comes to healing from an abusive relationship. And it's important to note that "no contact" includes more than just direct contact. I would also recommend blocking them on social media as well as asking mutual friends or other contacts to refrain from sharing things about them or messages from them.

If you disregard the no-contact rule in even a seemingly innocent way, you run the risk of getting sucked back into the manipulation. In the online support group, I saw so many stories of this from abused people who believed their abusers' manipulative tactics to get them back—only to find the same abusive behavior not long after they returned.

To combat that possibility, it was recommended to me—and I pass along the recommendation to you—to create a list of transgressions that your abuser committed during the course of the relationship that you can refer to if you ever think about going back to them. This prevents "euphoric recall," which is remembering only the good times and forgetting all the bad times. After a while away from the abuser, an abused person can become lonely and miss that person—conveniently (or inconveniently) forgetting everything that led them to leave in the first place. This list can be a helpful and preventive reminder.

Still, my relationship addiction continued even without contact—though to a lesser extent. I worried about him constantly and still felt like my happiness was contingent on his being happy. I felt like if I knew he moved on and was happy, then I would be free to be happy as well. It took time to process these feelings and let them go.

But I had taken one major step in the right direction toward taking care of myself, which was learning how to set boundaries. And cutting off all contact was one hell of a boundary!

In the months following my ex's admission to the ICU, I had set boundaries and threatened divorce multiple times, both to him and to his family. But when I finally made good on my threats, none of them could believe that I had actually gone through with it. "This just doesn't sound like Ted," they kept saying (from what I heard, anyway). They expected me to stay—to continue as I had always done—because that was all they knew, and I had never shown much of any evolution throughout the life of our relationship. So they were right—it didn't sound like me, because I had been reborn into a new version of myself.

Meanwhile, within a couple of months after I left my ex, I learned he was hospitalized three more times due to more seizure-related episodes. Because I wasn't there, I can't say with certainty what the underlying reasons for those hospitalizations were—although I have my reasonable suspicions since his history showed that alcohol use caused his seizure problems. Things hadn't changed; it was just more of the same.

Along those same lines, the divorce process was—as you might expect—a nightmare. I was annoyed by the demands from his side for an equal share in everything even though he hadn't contributed equally during the marriage (not to mention the abuse). The delays and lack of communication were frustrating to no end.

But again, the frustrations of the process were just more of the same of what I'd experienced throughout the relationship. It did make me regret ignoring my gut instinct to sign a prenuptial agreement prior to getting married—but then again, I didn't listen to my gut about marrying him in the first place, so why would I listen to my gut regarding any other aspect of the process?

I could put up with these frustrations, though. It was a breath of fresh air to *only* have to deal with a divorce! In contrast to the constant abusive thoughts and emotions of my relationship, the challenges of the divorce were finite. My new life had begun.

HOW DID I NOT SEE IT?

I've already mentioned why it took me so long to recognize my relationship as abusive, and why it took me so long to realize I needed to leave. But for most of our relationship, I also wasn't aware that he needed to seek help for his alcohol addiction. Blinders again, yes. But allow me to explain.

This may sound crazy, but I did not realize he was an alcoholic until he received that diagnosis in the ICU. I knew he drank too much, and I could see the negative impacts it had on his life and our relationship—but it never clicked for me that he was an addict. Sometimes we miss (or deny) things that later seem so obvious.

A big part of me did not want to admit the severity of his drinking problem. There's an important distinction between "drinking too much" and "being an alcoholic"—and it's difficult to take the leap from the first to the second, whether it's related to identifying yourself or someone close to you. We have a difficult time admitting that these things could happen to us. As both Alcoholics Anonymous (AA) and Al-Anon teach us, the first step of recovery is admitting we have a problem—and sometimes that can be the most difficult step.

My denial was partly due to ignorance about alcoholism. I did not realize that literally all of his health issues could be tied back to his overuse of alcohol and Xanax. (And, to be fair, the tie between alcoholism and seizures is rare.) I knew that the more he drank, the worse his seizure-related symptoms would get—but I still thought there was something else going on that the medical professionals hadn't figured out yet.

In addition, at the time, I understood an alcoholic to be someone who often exhibited typical drunk behavior like stumbling and slurring. My ex rarely acted like this—yet another reason why the term "alcoholic" never crossed my mind. *What I failed to realize was that someone with a high tolerance of alcohol can drink several times more than the average person and still not come across as drunk in the "usual" sense.* Instead, his consumption of alcohol resulted in different effects—those mental and physical symptoms I described before as "episodes" (e.g., dizziness, weakness, memory loss, head and body pain, mini-seizures).

Another factor in my denial and ignorance is that alcohol overuse is still such a normalized behavior in our society. Drinking a lot and often is something people can wear with a badge of honor and make so many jokes about—and few people bat an eye. I now have a hard time finding humor in all the memes floating around the internet about drinking alcohol being a "fun hobby" or necessity to get through the day. Alcohol is more dangerous than many people realize—significantly more harmful than most illegal drugs, in fact. Mental health and substance abuse are major issues that require increased attention and care in terms of how we approach them. And to me, they are not a joking matter.

Of course, these things are all clear to me now that I've emerged from the experience, but I'm sure many people feel trapped in a situation much like my own. I have a hard time bringing myself back to how I felt and what I thought during that time because so many things seem clear and obvious to me now. I have to remind myself how easy it is to fall into the trap of ignorance and delusion. It can take years to wake up, and some people never do.

However, just because it took me this long to come to my senses doesn't mean the same has to be true for you. I may be grateful for my experience, but I wouldn't wish that pain, trauma, sadness, anger, and debilitation on anyone. I want you to gain an awareness of your own situation and get the necessary help long before getting anywhere near what I experienced at rock bottom.

CAN A RELATIONSHIP SURVIVE ADDICTION?

The short answer: maybe.

Certainly, you can do like I did and "stick it out" with the addict—with no changes to the status quo—but this isn't healthy for you or your loved one. Things need to change, one way or another.

If you were thinking, "Oh, good! He's saying I don't have to end my relationship. I was getting really uneasy thinking that I'd have to have some uncomfortable conversations"—sorry to burst your bubble. If you want to be truly happy, you're ultimately going to have to confront these concerns within yourself and with the other person.

To reiterate my point from the previous chapter, if the addict is also a narcissist, sociopath, or psychopath, then my advice is to get the hell out and never look back.

On the other hand, if abuse is nonexistent or significantly less extreme, it's possible to make the relationship work—but with critical guidelines:

1. **Boundaries, boundaries, boundaries!** What do you need to feel safe? Most people need the addict to be completely clean in order to feel comfortable in the relationship. You'll also want to express how the other person can appropriately communicate with you, which brings us to . . .

2. **Communication.** Don't play guessing games with each other. Express how you feel, what your challenges are, and what you need from the other person. If you don't ask for what you need, the answer will always be no.

3. **Self-work—for both individuals.** In most cases, I would say this means that the addict attends regular AA meetings and the other attends Al-Anon meetings—or the equivalent for the addiction at hand. Therapy is also important for both individuals, as well as continued growth work on each person's own time. (If the addict refuses to participate in these activities, you'll have to decide for yourself whether this is acceptable—and if not, communicate a boundary. See how this all ties together?)

There is somebody for everybody. Not everyone is willing or able to go as deep on the healing journey as others, and that's okay. For some relationships, it may be acceptable for an addict to continue partaking in their addiction; for others, this may be a deal-breaker.

A word of warning: many addicts who are clean and sober from one substance will turn to other seemingly less harmful substances (like marijuana or food) or behavioral addictions (like shopping or exercising to an extreme) because they haven't done the work to address the underlying causes that led to the addictions in the first place.

When the addict continues to partake in their original addiction or finds a new addiction to replace it, the addict is incapable of being fully present or authentically themselves. Therefore, that individual is inherently incapable of having a truly healthy relationship (as defined later in this book) with anyone—including themselves. It is up to that person's partner and other people in their lives to decide whether to continue a relationship with someone who is physically and emotionally unable to be who they truly are.

Addiction also stunts emotional development. Beginning to use substances heavily (particularly in adolescence) causes problems with an individual's ability to experience normal adulthood—i.e., an advanced sense of wisdom, heightened understanding of consequences, and overall emotional maturity.[5] In other words, if someone starts drinking or using drugs as a teenager, their emotional maturity will remain at that level (or significantly stunted from advancement) until they become sober. (When I learned this, pretty much everything about my relationship with my ex made sense—I had been dealing with a teenager for fifteen years. It explained the focus on himself and disregard for or inability to perceive consequences of his actions.)

> "There's more to quitting drinking than quitting drinking."
>
> —DR. PAUL O.—

Recovery takes years and has to become a way of life. It takes full commitment from the addict, as well as support from loved ones, to achieve and maintain. As someone recovers, they can unwind the root causes as to why the addiction began in the first

5. Nikki Seay, "Can Early Drug Abuse Stunt Emotional Maturity?" American Addiction Centers, last modified November 4, 2019, https://www.rehabs.com/blog/does-adolescent-addiction-really-stunt-emotional-maturity/.

place—and from there, healthy relationships with themselves and other people can blossom.

GOING BEYOND THE BULLSHIT EXCUSES

Some people attempt the critical action items described in the previous section (boundaries, communication, and self-work)—and even get the other person in the relationship to join them—yet it doesn't work for one reason or another. Either only one person sticks with the game plan, or both people give up. One or both individuals return to the "comfort zone" of how things used to be, which they both know wasn't working in the first place.

Yet both people continue to stick around. Why is that?

Fear.

For example, as I discussed briefly in the previous chapter, people sometimes stay in unhappy, abusive, codependent relationships "for the kids" as an "unselfish" way of providing stability to their children. Although I've witnessed the journeys of many people with kids (including parents in abusive marriages), I don't have kids myself, so many people would likely argue that I'm not allowed to have an opinion—but I'm going to give it to you anyway.

Some parents think that if they avoid arguing in front of the kids, then the kids won't be emotionally impacted or realize what's going on. These parents fail to realize how perceptive kids are—they can pick up on the subtlest of cues, like muttering under the breath or even a quick facial expression. Even at a young age, they are intuitive enough to

> "Strength is removing your kids from a toxic environment. Not 'learning to live with it for the sake of the kids.'"
>
> —UNKNOWN—

sense the energy of those around them without any words being said or actions being taken.

In unhealthy situations that involve abuse or addiction, it is actually *more* selfish to allow the same family situation to continue. At the root of it, one or both parents' fear is what keeps them from making a change. Of course, this can happen regardless of whether kids are in the picture.

Fear often keeps people in relationships that are no longer healthy or mutually beneficial. They fear change; they fear ending up alone; they fear their inability to make things work on their own; and/or they fear not being able to find someone better.

1. **Fearing change** is a natural human phenomenon. We fear the unknown. Our current situation is our "comfort zone," even when it's full of unhappiness, which might make no sense—but it happens to a lot of us. We would rather remain in an unhappy situation because at least it's "the devil we know"—we know what to expect. What if this unknown future situation is worse?

2. **Fearing being alone** is another natural human feeling because we are designed to be in relationships with other people (whether romantic or otherwise). Now that I've gotten out of that toxic relationship, I would always opt for being alone over being unhappy in a relationship. I can create happiness on my own significantly more easily than I can in a relationship with a partner who doesn't want the same thing for himself or us. But some people would rather stay in an abusive relationship than end up alone because on some level, they're saying, "At least I have somebody to sleep next to."

3. **Fearing our inability to be independent** likely comes from never having proven to ourselves that we can do it. I get it—I had never lived alone prior to leaving my ex. My only advice here is to give yourself more credit. You'll figure things out, just like I did. And while trying new things in an abusive relationship usually ends in getting mocked, ridiculed, or even punished, the only person you have to answer to when you're on your own is yourself.

4. **Fearing our inability to find someone better for us** stems from a lack of self-worth. We believe the asshole we're with today is the best we can do. Who else would love us at this age, at this weight,

with this many kids, with all these quirks? "My partner may be a dick, but at least he stays with me. I won't be able to find anyone better, and even if I do, they probably won't stay with someone like me." Perhaps you're not thinking these exact words, but by believing you're unable to find someone better, you're essentially believing these statements. Come on! Would you talk to any of your close friends like this? No. Be kinder and more loving to yourself. You're more of a catch than you may realize.

Any combination of these fears may come into play. For me, I feared change and an inability to be independent. I did not fear being alone or an inability to find someone better. I knew I would rather be alone than continue to suffer in the relationship with him, and I had little doubt that I'd be able to find someone better.

In less intense situations of unhappiness, perhaps the family can stay together without long-term damage to each individual—for example, in situations where the parents are better friends than lovers and, therefore, get along quite well. But I believe that long-term toxic situations only teach children that it's okay for them to continue being miserable and not stand up for themselves or their happiness. In those cases, is staying together really sending the right message to them? Would you want them to be as miserable in their future as you may be now?

IN CLOSING

My experiences may seem like some extreme version of a story that could never happen to you. I've shared this all with you, though, to help you recognize potential warning signs in the early stages of abuse, addiction, or both. If you or your partner (or other loved one) struggle with these unhealthy behaviors to any degree, I urge you to increase your awareness of your current situation, communicate with each other, and potentially seek help if needed. (And remember—if those communications between the two of you lead to arguments full of accusations and defensiveness, that red flag is a-wavin'.)

You may also be wondering why I'm sharing all these details about my life. In my experience, the loved ones of addicts have much in common—so my guess is that if you fall into that category (whether you realize it yet or not), you can relate to some or most of my story. I want to ensure you are aware of the warning signs of addiction and codependency so that you can do something about your situation before it worsens.

Regardless of the type of addiction involved (e.g., alcohol, drugs, food, pornography) and regardless of the type of relationship, codependent thoughts, behaviors, and experiences include the following:

1. Dealing with denial, lies, and manipulation
2. Obsessing over how much addictive behavior the addict engages in (e.g., counting and measuring bottles)
3. Suspecting addictive behaviors happening behind our backs—and accusing the addict of such
4. Resorting to unhealthy and even addictive coping mechanisms ourselves
5. Attempting (but often failing) to process and understand their baffling words and behavior
6. Controlling or attempting to control the addict and our circumstances as much as possible
7. Being unable to establish and maintain clear, firm boundaries
8. Bearing the burden and frustration of watching someone we love self-destruct
9. Being the object of resentment
10. Feeling no gratitude or satisfaction (only resentment) for taking care of them and looking out for their best interests
11. Facing increasing difficulty with intimacy and connection (emotional, mental, and sexual)
12. Fearing for their lives as we lose our own sanity
13. Consuming our entire lives with the thoughts and actions described here with no time to take care of ourselves or simply take a break

If these characteristics resonate with you, I urge you to seek therapy or start attending Al-Anon meetings.

It is possible for a relationship to survive addiction, but healthy boundaries are critical. Ultimately, you will have to evaluate what is right for you—whether you feel safe, supported, respected, and loved.

Relationships should be an enhancement to our lives—not hold us back, or worse, make things unbearable. If we're unhappy in a relationship and stay in it out of fear, we're missing the point.

People mistakenly think that they have to be in a relationship in order to be happy. No, it's the other way around—we have to be able to find happiness by ourselves *in order to* be truly happy in a healthy relationship. Now, we can move on to discuss how to do that.

> "It's crazy when the thing we love the most is the detriment— let that sink in."
>
> —HALSEY, "GRAVEYARD"—

—REFLECTION—

How does addiction—your own or someone else's—impact you? What codependent behaviors do you exhibit in your relationships?

HEALING OURSELVES

What prevents us from being happy?

We tend to blame other people for our problems, but our problems really begin with us. This concept is difficult to look at and admit, which is why I ordered the book this way—focusing first on abuse- or addiction-related problems that arise within relationships before addressing internal problems. Those external challenges can be so significant that they make it impossible to even think about how we feel about ourselves.

Now, we can shift gears to focus on problems that reside within us, regardless of whether we're in a relationship with someone else. But as it turns out, our relationships with other people mirror our relationships with ourselves—so it's all interconnected. For example, if you don't value yourself, you will surround yourself with people who also don't value you, perhaps without even realizing it. You get what you give—or, in other words, you get from others what you give to yourself.

That's why we're now shifting to an inward focus. *By beginning to look within ourselves, we can start to heal old wounds.*

You may not feel like there is much to heal, but you might be surprised. Perhaps you've already ended a relationship with an abuser or addict, so you think your work is done and problems are behind you. However, the relationship still haunts you, or you keep attracting more of the same kinds of people. Why is that, and how do you fix that?

Or maybe you've never experienced a relationship that involved abuse or addiction, and you're wondering whether "this stuff" still applies to you. It does. We all have stuff from which to heal.

In this chapter, we'll cover what this kind of introspection and healing looks like. Fair warning: this process requires that we relive some painful, uncomfortable experiences to deal with our own shit, face our past, and feel our feelings—and yes, we'll get into what it means to "feel our feelings."

But not all of these healing experiences are unpleasant. Dealing with this emotional baggage helps us make room for joy and happiness in our lives. We will connect with others who help us along the way, and the connections we make with them will be strong and powerful. A whole new world opens up for us when we decide to own responsibility for our healing journey.

DEALING WITH OUR OWN SHIT

The first step in healing ourselves is to recognize that our current situation isn't working for us. As noted above, sometimes that means addressing our relationships with other people first. We've already discussed that ad nauseum—I think you've gotten the point by now.

However, at the root of these issues is what's going on inside us. Dealing with the truth of our inner struggles—and why we are the way we are—is critical to achieving that ultimate goal of finding happiness.

"Nobody else is responsible for your life but you. Many people may be at fault for your pain and unhappiness. But no one else is responsible for your digging you out of that pain or unhappiness."

—MARK MANSON—

To start us off, I'll discuss anxiety, depression, and sexuality—three of my journeys. To be clear, when I say our problems begin with us, I am not saying we are to *blame* for these experiences (nor is sexuality in and of itself a "problem"). However, I do believe it is our responsibility—and only our responsibility—to be aware of these things and work to get help on making things better for ourselves.

ANXIETY

I still experience quite a bit of anxiety, even as I write this book. In fact, I had written the first several paragraphs of this section when my laptop unexpectedly crashed and I lost my progress. I feel like that is no coincidence as I write to you about my experience with anxiety.

For me, anxiety manifests as some combination of chest tightness, shortness of breath or labored breathing, a pounding heart, shaky hands, or an inability to think clearly. These moments can appear seemingly out of nowhere—whether the current situation is stressful or calm. For other people, anxiety may manifest in different ways, including sweating, headaches, muscle aches and pains, loss of libido, increased blood pressure, or an upset stomach.

I learned recently that anxiety in and of itself can be an addiction. Our bodies and minds become so used to being on high alert all the time that it's difficult to break free of these patterns. Our brains get used to the combination of chemicals that are involved in our patterns of thinking and feeling.

For me, I believe a large part of my anxiety comes from perfectionism and being a high achiever. As a kid, achievement came so easily to me that I rarely celebrated those moments. On the flip side, I ruminated over anything that was less than perfection. Anything less than an A in school (sometimes even less than A+) was not acceptable. I remember having an A- on a midterm report card in fourth grade and being so nervous to show my parents—not because I expected punishment or disappointment from them but because I held myself to such high standards. As a nine-year-old.

I believe that's why I'm so list-oriented as an adult and constantly thinking of everything I "need" to do. I view those things as accomplishments and beat myself up when I feel behind on my list. (And I ended up attracting a partner who abused me over things he felt I wasn't doing right or well enough to his liking—see the parallel there? I still have more work to do on myself.)

Some days, though, anxiety presents itself as an intense feeling of having so much to do. But when I take a moment to really think about it, I realize my "list" is not actually that long and is totally doable. While the anxiety can sometimes be motivating, oftentimes it is counterproductive instead.

Anxiety can also be passed down from generation to generation. According to Healthline.com, "[A] 2017 review of studies concluded that generalized anxiety disorder (GAD) can be inherited, with GAD and associated conditions being linked to a number of different genes. Most researchers conclude that anxiety is genetic but can also be influenced by environmental factors."[6] Among other things, we inherit anxiety—often undiagnosed and untreated—from our parents, as well as from ancestors who go further back in our family lineage. As kids, we absorb ways of behaving and thinking from our home environment.

Some of my anxiety also comes from the C-PTSD from my past relationship. It shows up in my current relationships as triggers that often have little or nothing to do with what the person says or does, but the situation mirrors something from my past and I expect the familiar bad things from the past to repeat themselves.

The C-PTSD also shows up with various reminders of the relationship and its memories throughout any given day—for example, seeing photos from memories we shared (whether he's in the photo or not) or remembering the origin of various items throughout my house. It's weird how often I'm unfazed by these reminders—yet at other times, it will randomly manifest as tightness in my chest—a sensation I regularly experience and will explore further later in this chapter. In those moments, it can be difficult to break from the pain and trauma of those memories,

6. "Is Anxiety Genetic?" Healthline, accessed February 22, 2021, https://www.healthline .com/health/mental-health/is-anxiety-genetic.

which can be so strong that it's like reliving the experience all over again. This ties into the addiction to the relationship and its drama that I mentioned earlier.

My anxiety shows up the strongest when I am faced with confronting the experiences of that relationship in a deep, thoughtful way—in therapy, as an example. In those moments, my body and mind try to keep me safe from reliving the emotions and experiences associated with those memories.

What's important to remember is that anxiety always covers up some other emotion that is uncomfortable or even scary to feel—whether it's sadness, anger, or fear, for example.

The interesting yet confusing paradox of my anxiety is that it usually shows up in moments of relative calm and not necessarily in moments of crisis. While writing this book, one day I experienced a plumbing mess in my home where an upstairs bathroom leak caused water to fall through the floor and through my kitchen ceiling. I quickly addressed the problem and cleaned up the mess, but I remained calm throughout the process—a very different demeanor from the uncomfortable, jittery anxiety I experience when nothing immediately needs my attention.

This phenomenon comes from an inner protective measure that developed when I was a kid—a measure that, as an adult, came to my aid by keeping me as calm as possible during the fifteen years that I lived through total unpredictability. Because I was constantly on guard for so long, my body has not yet adapted to peacefulness. I am still on the path to curing my addiction to chaos.

Finally, anxiety also comes from an inability to be present, which is still an ongoing struggle for me. It is next to impossible for any of us to be present at all times; however, it is important to focus on the present as much as possible—and a complete inability to do this may signify other issues.

Are you able to pause in any given moment and just appreciate the present without any fears about the future or angst about the past? If you are never able to do this, you might suffer from anxiety as well. (And to be clear, you still may have anxiety even if you *are* able to do this from time to time.) Both the past and future are out of our control, so dwelling on either is futile and detracts from our ability to be in the moment. The present is the only time over which we have any control, and we can significantly reduce our level of anxiety if we focus only on what's in front of us.

Developing a regular meditation practice has been instrumental in reducing my anxiety. This was difficult at first—and is often still difficult—because of my tendency to overthink. However, meditation not only aids in our ability to be present but also allows us the opportunity to practice kindness to ourselves. *It is okay for our minds to wander while we meditate. Just notice it and bring your focus back to the present.* I recommend trying a guided five-minute meditation to get started, and from there you can expand to longer sessions or unguided meditations. (I provided a list of options in the back of the book.) I also recommend trying different settings—indoors versus outdoors, as an example. Different approaches work for different people, but I believe meditation is a good practice for everyone.

Medication is also an option to treat symptoms of anxiety. I'll preface all of this by saying that I am not a medical expert, and you should consult your physician on this topic. Prescription drugs or herbal remedies (or a combination) can help. You have to find what works for you. However, my (non-medical) understanding is that these prescription and herbal remedies tend to treat the symptoms of anxiety rather than get at the root of what's causing the symptoms in the first place. So if you choose to utilize these options, my recommendation is to still do the work to address the underlying cause so that your anxiety can be *cured*, not simply treated.

You may be surprised by what you discover on this journey of reducing overthinking and focusing on the present moment. For example, one day I went for a run on my usual route through nearby neighborhoods. On one street, all the driveways were perpendicular to the street, but that day I noticed for the first time that one driveway met the street at an angle. I had run past this spot dozens of times before but never noticed this bit of uniqueness.

This was a reminder to me that when we're able to be truly present and observe our surroundings—rather than being caught in mind chatter about the past or the future—we're able to notice more about the world around us. We see things we didn't see before. We develop insights that we didn't know were in us. And we can be more at peace.

DEPRESSION

Although undiagnosed at the time I was going through it, I experienced situational depression, which occurs when a person develops certain emotional symptoms that are more exaggerated than normal in response to a stressful life situation.

This differs from clinical depression, which is more severe and can interfere with daily function. Clinical depression can be caused by disturbances with neurotransmitters, genetic factors, major life events, or alcohol and drug dependence.[7]

I wanted to call out these differences before sharing my experience with depression. However, although these differences exist, often the manifestations are similar—and both types of depression are important to address.

As those years of my relationship went by, I began to feel like a shell of a human being. I was emotionless, all my energy drained. Things lost color and just had a grayness to them. I lost my identity. I lost hope. I had very little motivation to do any household chores beyond the bare minimum needed to get through the day, which I accomplished simply by going through the motions. (And there's a cycle here related to lack of motivation: depression leads to a lack of activity, which can lead to worsened depression because nothing is getting done, and then the body continues to remain inactive.) I did not have any direction or goals. It was so hard to get out of bed, and I just wanted to sleep all day every day. Some days I cried all alone while other days I just sat and stared. Everything just sucked.

Life had very little meaning. I found myself thinking things like:
Is this all there is?
How did I get here?

7. Valencia Higuera, "Situational Depression or Clinical Depression?" *Medical News Today*, September 28, 2018, https://www.medicalnewstoday.com/articles/314698.

What's the point of even trying?

I felt worthless, unfulfilled, and futureless.

I also felt alone and that no one would understand. I didn't realize how many other people were suffering silently just as I was—someone just next door could have been in the same boat. Depression is more common than we sometimes realize. We feel disconnected because feelings of isolation are one of the symptoms of depression. This leads to a downward spiral—depression disconnects us from others, which only leads to worsened depression.

Because my depression was not as severe as what so many others experience, I was functional in most senses of the word. I doubt anyone in my life knew what was going on inside. My work ethic generally didn't slip; in fact, work was something easy to focus on. And I kept my relationships going as best I could, partly so I could keep up the façade that everything was okay. This was overwhelming and quite draining since I already had such little energy.

Why would someone settle for a life like this? This may surprise you as someone on the outside looking in, but if you've experienced or are experiencing these feelings, you'll get it: *it can feel like things will never get better.* With all or most hope lost, it can feel like this is all there is going to be for the rest of your life. It feels like a trap from which there is no escape.

So how do we cure this disease?

I can tell you a few things that sure as hell *don't* work—the first being alcohol. As you know by now, I drank way too much, which only made my depression worse. As shocking as this may sound, *depressants don't alleviate depression.*

There are plenty of other things we call "Band-Aids," which only temporarily cover up the issue but don't actually heal or fix the problem. This includes various addictive behaviors such as drugs, smoking, overeating, excessive screen time, or gambling.

We will talk about approaches that do work, but first, a caveat: this book is not meant to be a tool for therapy—only to guide you in the right direction. If you are experiencing symptoms like I've described in this section, I highly recommend you seek professional help. I've been relieved to see how the stigma toward mental health issues has been reduced in recent years, but I recognize there may still be some hesitation on your part to talk to someone. Trust me, there is nothing to be ashamed of—more people than you perhaps realize have experienced the same or similar feelings you have. You are not alone.

If you're going through depression, therapy is the best place to be, though I actually feel that therapy could benefit everyone—even those who are doing well in their lives. It's a safe place to talk through problems and get answers (sometimes just by saying things out loud and reaching your own conclusions, even without advice from the counselor).

One bit of advice relative to therapy: if your counselor gives you homework assignments, do them. The voice of your inner critic inside your head will tell you they're stupid or they won't work, but trust the process. What's the worst that can happen? Don't try to tell me they're a waste of time when we both know you waste your time in plenty of other ways!

If you're concerned about the cost of therapy due to the lack of good (or any) insurance, I still recommend exploring. Many therapists have a graduated pay scale to work with low-income individuals. If therapy is ultimately too cost-prohibitive, there are free support groups for all sorts of different topics. Refer to the back of this book for a few examples.

But if you can make it work, therapy will be the best money you've ever spent. You should be your own biggest investment anyway! You'll be surprised how other aspects of your life start coming together once you focus on bettering yourself.

Another piece of advice: *It's very important that you feel a good connection with your therapist. Not everyone is for everyone. If you aren't clicking or don't get a good vibe from one therapist, find a new one.* This is an important investment in yourself, and it's critical that you find a good fit. Don't let one negative experience with a therapist dictate your viewpoint on therapy in general.

In my case, I happened to heal from my depression without going to therapy and only started working with my therapist after the fact. But I wish I had had her at that time—that's for sure.

Like with anxiety, medication can also help treat symptoms of depression, and again, find what works for you. Your therapist can help you navigate this, too, even if they don't prescribe medication. And as I said before, I do believe that medication should go hand in hand with therapy to ensure you're getting to the underlying reasons for the condition rather than just treating symptoms.

For me, my most significant step in the right direction toward getting better was to cut back significantly on my alcohol intake. If you feel like you might be depressed and are also a regular drinker, I recommend that you reevaluate your drinking habits.

Other healthy activities that help reduce symptoms and effects of depression include physical activity (I personally love to run!), reading, laughing, and celebrating small wins.

I'd also encourage you to open up and share what you're going through with a trusted family member or friend—while keeping in mind that these individuals are not professionals and shouldn't be relied upon as such. If depression worsens with lack of connection, then connecting with loved ones is a great way to combat those symptoms.

I've also had the benefit of working with life coaches. There are some great advantages to concurrently working with both a therapist and a life coach. A therapist will help you get at the root of your problems while a life coach will give you that extra push to motivate yourself and achieve your goals. Because of this important distinction, if you're experiencing symptoms of depression or other mental health conditions, I highly recommend working with a therapist over a life coach. You can certainly do both, but therapy is where you need to head to work through those specific issues.

SEXUALITY

In my case, being gay has a lot to do with how my thoughts and feelings developed over the years into adulthood. And I think many LGBTQ+ individuals can relate to aspects of this story.

I grew up in a small town in southern Illinois. My family was loving and supportive, but I was also very sheltered as a kid—to the extent that I didn't even know gayness was "a thing." For several years, I just knew I was different from all the other kids, but I couldn't pinpoint why.

In the end, it was other kids who clued me in to my own identity by teasing me for being gay. I'm guessing that started when I was nine or ten years old. I hit puberty early—I remember shaving stubble off my face in fourth grade—so of course I got teased for that, too. I felt different from other kids even before hitting puberty, but that's when my attraction to the same sex started to develop.

However, even though I got my first clues from childhood bullies, I still was relatively clueless about what it meant to be gay. I grew up in the Catholic Church, which has official stances on homosexuality, but these are rarely discussed at weekend services or even in the curriculum taught in Catholic middle schools like the one I attended.

At age thirteen, I developed a strong friendship with a girl in the class ahead of mine, and we ended up dating for almost four years. I had loving feelings and even physical attraction toward her, which further confused me because I thought I might be gay before I met her. I continued in the relationship, and the feelings toward her progressed, but the gayness didn't go anywhere, either.

After approximately one year into our relationship, I decided to tell my girlfriend that I thought I might be gay. I hadn't shared this with anyone else at this point. In my mind, she was the closest person to me, and I was looking for support and understanding. I'm not sure how I thought this expectation could be realistic; understandably, when the guy she'd been dating for almost a year told her he might be gay, she did not react well. In fact, I had my first experience with how someone can feel homosexuality is sinful and disgusting.

It was not my first experience with rejection because I had certainly experienced plenty of moments of exclusion and feeling unwanted by my peers. However, it was my first experience with rejection from someone I trusted and loved.

Because I loved her and wanted to continue a relationship with her, I agreed to try to "fix" myself and turn straight. And because she loved me and wanted to continue a relationship with me, she tried to "help." As you can imagine, this was no easy task—impossible tasks usually aren't all that easy. It was one thing to hide myself and pretend I was something I was not for kids in my class so that I could avoid being teased and ostracized. It was a whole new ballgame to have to hide who I was from someone whom I truly loved. I wasn't able to change a part of myself that I thought was wrong, which brought on some really dark feelings of shame, self-loathing, and self-rejection.

Those feelings toward the self are common within the LGBTQ+ community. Within the gay community specifically, there is so much internalized and externalized homophobia because of the shame we feel about who we are. We often project that shame outward onto other people within our own community—saying someone is "too gay," "too feminine" (in the case of a man), or "too masculine" (in the case of a woman).

These feelings of shame and our often-challenging experiences with coming out are likely a significant source of the prevalent anxiety and depression that exist within the LGBTQ+ community.

My girlfriend and I did a lot of talking and processing together and experienced successes and failures together. We ultimately spent a total of nearly four years together in a relationship, by the end of which I had drawn the conclusion that I was bisexual. I had little to no physical attraction to other females, but she was the exception. We both felt good about this conclusion because it meant we could still be together while still allowing myself to be attracted to other guys.

We ended our relationship on the friendliest of terms—not over my sexuality, but just as a peaceful sunset on that chapter of our lives. And sixteen years later, we are closer than ever. I am eternally grateful for our friendship and the journey we went through together.

Shortly after the end of that relationship, I realized that I was not bisexual; I was—I am—gay (with maybe a sprinkle of bisexuality). This was an easier transition to come to terms with once I was out of the relationship with that girlfriend because the change wouldn't affect her. (Hey there, codependency—good to see you again.)

My journey with sexuality had a significant impact on shaping me (and her, too). Her reaction when I came out to her made me fear future rejection from other close relationships in my life; I didn't know how I could tell my family or other friends, no matter how safe I felt with any of them.

While I had begun to accept my sexuality, my process of figuring it out had a lasting impact on me. During that time, I had developed a strong rejection and hatred for myself. I didn't want to be gay; I didn't want to be different. Essentially, I didn't want to be myself.

Meanwhile, I also continued to criticize myself regularly because of high standards. And I lacked self-worth. I may not have consciously told myself I wasn't worthy, but those feelings were there at least subconsciously.

> "You teach people how to treat you."
>
> —MAYA ANGELOU—

These feelings and fears led to an unhealthy relationship with myself, which ultimately—only three months after ending the relationship with that girlfriend—led me into a fifteen-year relationship with someone who treated me just like I treated myself.

A couple of months into that relationship, I was blessed to have one of the easiest coming out experiences with my family that I've ever heard of within the LGBTQ+ community. I still was not 100 percent comfortable with myself and needed external validation that it was okay from those I was closest to (both family and friends). Not everyone accepted me unconditionally, but generally speaking, I had it relatively easy. The challenges and heartache that many individuals experience with coming out were not part of my story. Different challenges were on their way.

To anyone struggling with their own or others' acceptance of their sexual orientation or gender identity, I'd encourage you to reach out to your local LGBTQ+ community. The Trevor Project and the It Gets Better Project are great resources for LGBTQ+ youth, and PFLAG is wonderful for parents of LGBTQ+ individuals. These organizations can help you find safe, healthy ways of connecting with other LGBTQ+ individuals in your area.

GETTING HELP (SO WE CAN DEAL WITH OUR SHIT)

Those are a few examples of the issues I had to face in myself. I dealt with the depression and became comfortable with my sexuality well before I began therapy. My anxiety has been an ongoing challenge that I continue to work on personally and with the support of my therapist and coaches.

There may be other internal issues that require attention—for example, grief, shame, or uncontrolled anger. All of these internal challenges often come from unresolved pain and trauma. They can manifest in ways that create problems not only for ourselves but also in our relationships with other people.

Therefore, it's important to address these problems. How do we do that? Well, I'm so glad you asked.

THE HEALING JOURNEY

In order to improve the health of our relationships with others and ourselves, we have to connect with ourselves on a deep level to heal. Otherwise, we run the danger of past pain continuing to repeat itself. The work is not at all easy but is nonetheless essential to finding and maintaining joy and happiness.

If you are nearing the end of or are coming out of an unhealthy relationship like I've been describing in the previous chapters, I highly recommend finding a therapist who is well-experienced in working with clients who are or have been in relationships that involve abuse and addiction. The same is true even if—okay, *especially* if—you're smack-dab in the middle of an unhealthy relationship with no end in sight. Therapy will be a critical component of your recovery.

"The greatest achievement of humanity is not its works of art, science, or technology, but the recognition of its own dysfunction, its own madness."

—ECKHART TOLLE—

You may have heard a phrase like "doing the work on yourself to heal" and haven't been sure what that meant—I'm here to help explain. In addition, you may hesitate at the sound of doing "work," which I understand as well. The journey can certainly have its challenges, but it's

> "You've mastered survival mode. Now it is time to live."
>
> —DENISE KECHO—

nothing like surviving through an abusive relationship. That constant state of fight-or-flight is exhausting and traumatizing. Healing from it takes time, but the freedom, love, and relief we feel just from leaving a toxic situation are well worth the healing journey that follows.

I like to explain "doing the work" as the emotional equivalent of exercise for the physical body. There can be resistance to getting started—not only in beginning a steady regimen but also along the way. And it may not always be enjoyable when doing it. But our hearts, minds, and souls benefit the same way from doing this work as our physical bodies benefit from exercise. In both cases, we feel (and even look) better. We have more energy and zest for life.

When I first began therapy, I learned that one of the most important first steps for a rescuer like me was to start doing self-care activities. We hear a lot of about "self-care," but it's not always clear what that means. It should go beyond pampering (spa days as an example—though don't get me wrong, these can also be very helpful!) and include things like the following:

1. Taking time alone to breathe or meditate
2. Taking care of the physical body with good nutrition
3. Reducing or eliminating toxins in the body (unhealthy food, drugs, alcohol)
4. Journaling
5. Connecting with nature
6. Exercising
7. Getting professional help

Self-care can mean taking a break from everything, or it can include activities that help us grow, heal, and transform. Personally, because I love efficiency, I love to combine the activities listed above—for example, hiking or running on a nature trail with a break halfway to journal and meditate. Running is a decompressing release for me while journaling and meditating allow for introspection and evolution.

Ideally, that therapist you find should also be familiar, licensed, and experienced in the techniques of hypnotherapy and breathwork. These have been instrumental in helping me heal from the trauma that I experienced in my life, not only from that fifteen-year abusive relationship but also from childhood trauma.

You may not think you experienced anything traumatic as a kid—at least nothing as awful as what we see on television or in the news. I thought that, too. I was fortunate to have a childhood free from any abuse or significantly life-altering events. My parents are still happily married after fifty-five years, and my family of seven (plus in-laws, nieces, and nephews) has been relatively free of drama and has always gotten along fairly well.

But it's next to impossible for children to not experience any trauma. We as children experience defining moments that have a significant impact on us, which result in the creation of new beliefs about ourselves. Ultimately, these moments lead to our experiences as adults.

Perhaps in your case, you were forgotten at home or separated from a parent at a store. Maybe you witnessed or experienced a car accident. It could be things as "simple" as someone calling you ugly, stupid, fat, or weird for the first time or in an especially life-altering way. All these events can impact a child's mind and heart permanently.

Allow me to give you a couple of examples from my childhood.

At age four, I walked with my dad to our town park on a weekday as we had done many times. We played as we normally did, and at one point my dad decided to use the restroom but didn't tell me that's where he was going (or I didn't hear him say so). There I stood, seemingly alone in the park. I thought he had left me. My four-year-old mind thought maybe he walked home without me, so I decided to walk home by myself. And I did—a whole quarter mile or so. I remember crossing the busy two-lane highway in front of our house and looking to my left to see my dad about three hundred feet away, running to catch up with me. And that's all I remember.

Through hypnotherapy, I've been able to revisit that experience and tune into the thoughts and emotions I had in the moment. It was that day that I lost my innocence. And in the moment of looking around, unable to find my dad, I drew a life-changing conclusion: "I am alone."

The subconscious belief that I am alone carried through much of my life, and so much made sense when I pieced things together. It could explain why I never connected with other kids my age throughout most of middle school and junior high. It could explain why I found myself in a four-year relationship with a girl in high school—someone I did love deeply but could never love completely (because there was one, uh, critical component missing). My belief that I was alone could explain why I've always preferred independence in school and at work. And finally, it could explain why I was drawn to a relationship with a man with whom I'd spend fifteen years but never truly feel connected or loved. We may have been together, but I was very much alone.

Another childhood event at age five involved two other boys with whom I was playing on a swing set. One kid shoved me, either down or off the slide, and I landed on and fractured my wrist. Understandably, given the pain that followed, I began to cry. But the boys weren't having it—they teased, ridiculed, and laughed at me. I drew a conclusion that I cannot express how I feel without repercussions and that I have to deal with things on my own.

The conclusion set in so fast and strong that it took until the next day for my mom to know something was wrong because I never told her or my dad. Instead, she saw me holding my wrist close to my chest and had to draw out of me what was going on before rushing me to the hospital. This hesitation or complete unwillingness to express my feelings carried through to adulthood.

Hypnotherapy helps us then draw new conclusions, connect with and give love to the inner child within us who experienced those traumas, and release the old beliefs and potentially still-lingering thoughts and emotions. Here are my old and new conclusions:

OLD CONCLUSIONS	NEW CONCLUSIONS
I am alone.	I am surrounded by love; I am connected to others and myself.
It is unsafe for me to express how I feel without repercussions.	I am safe to express my emotions in a healthy manner.
I have to deal with things on my own.	I can ask for help when I need to.

Developing these new beliefs won't correct everything in a single session, but it gets us on the right path. For example, to this day, I am still working on improving my ability and willingness to express how I feel, especially in a moment of conflict. And dealing with things on my own is my safety zone—how I've historically processed my emotions. But I'm improving in both of these areas.

The more introspective work we do, the more insights we'll discover. As you know by now, I was very much a rescuer with my ex. But I soon learned that was not the first time I took on this role.

When I was born (eleven years after my next oldest sibling—surprise!), my dad was going through a dark time, having lost his job. A new baby in the house gave him someone toward whom to pour all his attention, love, and affection. It gave him new life. While this may sound sweet and heartwarming, I realized through a new lens that—holy shit—*I was born a rescuer.*

It can be quite alarming to realize how far back these roles and subconscious beliefs go—like to when we were newborns as in my case, but they can even go back to being in the womb. Some people, for example, were unwanted from the moment they were conceived and go through much or all of their lives feeling this.

Things that upset us the most are often less about the event in the present and more about something that happened as a child. For example, getting interrupted or dismissed in adulthood could trigger moments of being ignored as a child. If our reaction to something is overly emotional or borderline hysterical, then we are likely reliving a past event or experiencing some unresolved, residual feelings from it. Hypnotherapy can assist in getting at the root of these triggers and healing the original source of the thought or feeling.

> "If it's hysterical, it's historical"
>
> —UNKNOWN—

It's important to remember that only we are responsible for how we feel. Other people may say or do something hurtful, but it's our reaction to that hurtful behavior that causes our emotion to it. The way we react to situations holds all the power. Placing the blame and responsibility for our feelings on other people reinforces our victimhood and disempowers us.

Our inner child can appear in unhealthy ways during our adult life when we aren't getting our needs met. I recently watched videos from several years ago of a game night with my circle of friends, including my ex and me. Initially, I cringed at how drunk, loud, and obnoxious I was in an attempt to amuse my friends. However, through a new lens, I saw my inner child acting out—reacting from repressed negative emotions and seeking external validation from people he loved.

Breathwork is another powerful way to release tension and heal. There are various techniques that involve active breathing in a specific rhythm and style, which can result in all sorts of different sensations, visions, and emotions.

I've had some of my biggest breakthroughs and hardest healing cries during breathwork sessions. These have probably helped me the most in terms of healing from the relationship with my ex. The process helped me evolve from a place of feeling pity, anger, and disrespect toward him to a place of compassion and forgiveness.

The processes also helped me realize that the compassion and forgiveness I wanted to feel toward my ex were mirrors of what I needed to show toward myself. All along, that relationship with him—over those fifteen years and even now as I travel this healing journey—has been a mirror of the relationship I have with myself.

> "Forgive those who didn't know how to love you. They were teaching you how to love yourself."
>
> —RYAN ELLIOTT—

If you have the means to participate in an intensive group therapy program that includes hypnotherapy and breathwork, I strongly recommend you pursue these opportunities. They will allow you to heal from these traumas and subconscious beliefs that hold you back from living a true, full life. You'll be amazed at how dramatically your life will change for the better after going through the processes.

Recently, I've begun doing work to acknowledge what I took from my ex and how I hurt him. This is not easy work; we usually want to rationalize our behavior rather than admit our faults and shortcomings. Hypnotherapy has helped me realize how I contributed to the chaos of our relationship, enmeshed his identity with mine, and prevented him from taking ownership of his own life. This is part of what is called "shadow work" and is still a work in progress for me even as I type this. Some examples of how I harmed him include:

1. **My overthinking and obsession with needing to control** prevented me from being present and prevented both of us from feeling free.
2. **My perfectionism, attachment to outcomes, and belief there was only one right way of doing things** did not allow me to accept him for who he was.
3. **Being in love with his potential**—a version of him that did not exist—meant the relationship that I had was with a false reality instead of with him, which meant he was left alone.

Doing this kind of work allows us to come to a place of stronger love and acceptance for ourselves and who we are at our core. It can be messy and difficult at times but is necessary for truly taking care of ourselves.

However, while it is important that we continue this work on ourselves to achieve higher levels of peace and happiness, *it is also critical that we love and accept ourselves for where we are in the present moment.* This can be difficult when we see a light at the end of the tunnel and know there are better things waiting for us at the other end. I have had a tendency to attempt rushing my healing journey without appreciating where I am and how far I've come. This subconsciously trains my mind and heart to believe that where I am in the present is not acceptable.

What I've learned is the importance of treating myself with the same amount of kindness, patience, compassion, and understanding as I give to others. Doing so allows the healing journey to continue in a more profound and transformational way.

I've included a couple of journaling activities in the next few sections for you to reflect on certain things (*cue your groan or eyeroll*). Just do it! What do you have to lose? It's best to write your responses by hand, but if you insist on typing them or just thinking about your responses to your-self, I can deal with that. Here's your first one.

—ACTIVITY—

1. What self-care activities do you currently do? How often do you do them? Is that sufficient?
2. What would you like to add, change, or improve with respect to your self-care practices?

RELEASING BLOCKS BY FEELING OUR FEELINGS

I've battled with many issues around self-confidence. Much of that stems from an abusive ex who wore me down in that regard, but I had issues with confidence prior to that, too. I grew up in a sheltered environment where I wasn't exposed much to the world around me, which resulted in my naiveté and lack of common sense. When others considered some things to be common knowledge and I had no clue about them, I felt like I didn't know anything and was fearful of doing or saying the wrong thing.

Therapy and coaching have done wonders for my confidence, yet I recognize there is still significant room for growth. One thing that has changed, though, is knowing I have it in me to make the improvement happen. This opens up my mind and heart to allow that growth and expansion.

My point? Once you free your mind from the fog of unhappiness and lack of clarity, there is a whole new world for you to experience, one you may have never known existed. It's pretty great. Life is good when you figure out how to release pain and fear.

So how do you release pain and fear? It's all about sitting with those feelings. When this concept was first introduced to me, I didn't understand it at all. "Sit with my feelings"? "Allow myself to feel"? What the hell does that mean?

It means that when unpleasant feelings like fear, anger, or sadness come up, don't stifle them or distract yourself with something else. (Examples: "Oh, I'm feeling really sad, so I need to eat some ice cream," or "This anger is really uncomfortable—I need to ignore it and distract myself with happier things like TV.")

Instead, allow yourself to feel those emotions, however uncomfortable this may be. Notice where in your body the feeling manifests itself, as well as how it feels physically—perhaps it's an emptiness, heaviness, tightness, sharpness, or numbness. For me, as an example, I often experience tightness in my chest due to any variety of emotions I may be feeling.

When you allow your body to sit with these emotions and sensations and really focus on them, it allows you to then release the underlying feelings. You may also uncover new, unexpected emotions that were hiding underneath those feelings. (I'll share an example of that in the next section.)

We have a tendency to avoid or stifle feelings that are uncomfortable, but the feelings aren't the problem—they're there to give us information. Even though they can be uncomfortable, we should welcome them and sit with them so we can understand what is going on. If we acknowledge them, we'll heal, process, and feel better in the long run. If we ignore them, they're bound to show up with stronger or more serious physical sensations—even illness.

These are merely suggestions for you to begin exploring. Again, I strongly encourage seeking professional help to explore these techniques in a controlled, safe environment. Counselors and therapists can help you explore and understand your emotionally painful feelings, some of which may even show up as a persistent bodily sensation that cannot be explained medically.

Your mind and body will likely resist these techniques at first, but that is your subconscious attempting to protect you from bringing uncomfortable feelings to the surface. That's why it's so important to work through releasing these feelings in a safe environment so that you can ultimately heal not only the emotional discomfort but also any physical ailments tied to the feelings.

Sound weird to you? I don't blame you. But these techniques are proven to work. If you're like me, you might feel somewhat open to doing whatever "wacky" solutions might work—but still a little skeptical and uncomfortable about trying something unfamiliar. I get that. But think about other moments in your life when you tried something totally new to you and you ended up having an incredible experience. Something tells me this stuff can and will fall into that same category for you.

Healing processes with a trusted therapist or in a group setting are important. *While we're responsible for doing the work on ourselves, we can't do the work alone. Self-help activities on our own aren't even a fraction as effective as therapeutic activities with qualified professionals and a strong support system.*

My friend and fellow author Britt East wrote, "There is a paradox at play here: we are all in this together, but nobody can do it for us. Our personal growth and development journey starts with our individual efforts, our transformation. We may join with others in benevolent witness, but this work is ours alone. Even when we collaborate, we bring our personal work to the table. There it becomes the foundation for shared experience, learning, and growth. Our personal work is the soil in which the roots of the community tree are planted, fostered, and fixed. If we cease the work, the tree will wither and wane."[8]

Time for another journaling activity. If this one is too strenuous, uncomfortable, or confusing—or if you have more negative things to say about your life than positive—then you might want to consider getting therapy. Only you have the power to choose happiness and make your life better. And when I say "choose happiness," I don't mean some sort of light switch that you can simply flick on and be good to go. Nor can anyone else flip a switch for you. You can get help from experts who can guide you on this journey, but you yourself have to do the work. The first step can be scheduling that initial appointment. But for now, let's do some journaling.

---

8. Britt East, *A Gay Man's Guide to Life* (Houndstooth Press, 2020); used with permission.

—ACTIVITY—

Write down ten things regarding how you feel about the current state of your life. If you're single, how do you feel about that? If you're in a relationship, how do you feel about that? How are things going in general? How do you feel about your other relationships, your job, your finances, etc.? In general, how do you view your life on a daily basis?

EMBRACING JOY AND HAPPINESS

Before we dive into this discussion, let's talk about the important distinction between joy, happiness, and pleasure. All of these are wonderful to experience but are very different from each other. Others outside of this book may define the terms differently, so for purposes of our discussion, I want to make sure we're on the same page.

Joy is relatively consistent and is cultivated internally. It comes when we make peace with who we are, why we are, and how we are. Joy can also manifest when witnessing or achieving selflessness and feeling spiritually connected to a higher power or to other people.

Meanwhile, happiness is also a relatively consistent feeling but tends to be externally sourced and is based on other people, things, places, thoughts, and events. Longer-term happiness often results from choosing to be a kind, caring, compassionate and gentle person with ourselves and others.

Both joy and happiness can coexist with feelings of sadness, anger, and fear. Joy and happiness are constants while the others are temporary.

On the other hand, pleasure is a momentary feeling that comes from something external—good food, runner's high, having sex, and so on. Pleasure has to do with the positive experiences of our senses and with good things happening. This momentary good feeling does not last long because it is dependent upon external events and experiences. In order to keep up the feeling of pleasure, many people become addicted to these external experiences (e.g., food, exercise, sex, drugs, alcohol, money)—so we have to be careful about how much we rely on pleasure to make us feel good. That can be difficult when pleasure is so much easier to create than happiness and joy, which take a lot more work to cultivate and maintain.

Pleasure can also come in the avoidance of pain. That was the case for me. I knew how horrible the abuse felt, so I did everything in my power to prevent it from happening—even if doing so meant I would pay for it later, when things would inevitably blow up one way or another. As an example, I avoided confrontation at all costs—only to have things blow up later. *In choosing to avoid pain for the sake of our temporary emotional state, we sacrifice our longer-term happiness and emotional and mental well-being.*

I'm not saying pleasure is a bad thing. However, we need to be thoughtful about how and when we seek it. Constantly seeking pleasure or avoiding pain in an effort to feel good all the time is not healthy. Those challenging, more uncomfortable emotions of sadness, anger, and fear will come around to hit us eventually—and the longer we avoid them, the harder they'll hit.

Now, I have three questions for you to consider:

1. What brings you joy?
2. What makes you happy?
3. What gives you pleasure?

There are certainly simple pleasures in life to appreciate; for me, these are things like chocolate (the darker, the better!), sushi, sleeping in, the sound of my cats purring, a well-performed live theater production, and the rush of dopamine from completing a task.

What's interesting, though, is that those things used to be all I would look forward to in a given day because everything else was so stressful or difficult. I would savor those moments because I felt like they were all I had. Now, on the other hand, I have so many good things going on in my life that I have to remind myself to be present and enjoy those simple things. These little nuggets are what enhance a life that is already good.

Some people are in such a dark, difficult place that they cannot even recognize and appreciate these simple pleasures. And when asked the question of what brings them happiness or joy, they simply cannot answer. This is not only a challenging place to exist but an even more challenging one from which to move on. If you struggled to answer any of the three questions above, I encourage you to pause, reflect on this challenge, and consider getting help.

In my prior relationship, joy and long-term happiness were foreign concepts. Instead, I latched onto momentary spurts of happiness when I could breathe a temporary sigh of relief from ongoing pain, frustration, sadness, and hurt. Sometimes these moments were those rare, precious times that he and I would get along, but more often I found happiness in those moments of peace I could experience by myself or away from home.

I envied those whom I perceived to have the luxury of experiencing joy and happiness. I was perplexed by these concepts that felt so far out of my reach. I felt they had been stolen from me. In reality, I had allowed happiness to escape. And honestly, I'm not sure I had ever experienced joy at that point because I hadn't done any work on myself yet.

Happiness began to return to my life once I ended that relationship. I'll never forget being out for a run one random day, feeling peaceful and content, and thinking, "Wow, is this what it's like to be happy? This is awesome!" Like . . . who knew? But there was still more work to do; there was more to my healing journey ahead.

Within a few months of leaving my ex, I began to experience tightness in my chest on a regular basis. Fortunately, I knew intuitively from the beginning it was nothing physically serious but rather a sensation having to do with anxiety. I had numerous conversations with my therapist and life coaches to try and get at the source, which helped but would only temporarily reduce the tightness.

Months later, I began an intensive group therapy experience that met over the course of several months. There, I learned that anxiety covers up other feelings that are hiding underneath—often anger or sadness, which made sense to me. And I certainly had those feelings. But after a few different attempts using hypnotherapy, I finally uncovered another layer and discovered the ultimate source of that anxiety and chest tightness, which was totally unexpected: *a fear of joy and happiness.*

And then it all made sense. When I was in that relationship, happiness was scarce and usually short-lived. I would latch onto a few hours of getting along with my ex in the hope it would go on forever. Unfortunately, that time would soon be cut short with another fight, guilt trip, or hurtful comment—all of which served as yet more reminders that extended periods of happiness could not exist in my life. I cautioned myself with feelings of happiness because when I did allow them, they would always end abruptly and without warning. In other words, *moments of happiness signaled to me that unhappiness was soon on its way.*

Joy, on the other hand, was a new experience for me. Because I had started doing the work on myself to heal, I was beginning to discover it—and my body wasn't used to this yet. It was reacting in fear of the unknown.

After discovering my fear of joy and happiness in hypnotherapy, I had one of the most powerful emotional releases of my life as I shifted immediately from hypnotherapy to breathwork—some of the most tears I've shed at one time (at least that I can remember). And sure enough, following that experience, my chest tightness reduced by approximately 95 percent. The body-mind-heart-soul connection is powerful.

Since then, not only has happiness returned more strongly for me, but I've also discovered what it's like to feel joy and not be afraid of it. And now, I feel my joy is impenetrable. I don't even really fear losing this state because I don't feel that it's possible. Like I said, this unchanging state does not mean I don't get sad or angry—quite the opposite—but those emotions can coexist with joy. And let me tell you what—how I'm feeling now is pretty awesome and not something I'm going to let go.

I've also found new sources of happiness that I did not know existed for me—like cooking, which I did not do for fifteen years in my relationship (and very little before that as well) because I feared being ridiculed for making mistakes. As it turns out, I am kind of a natural! Again, who knew?

I've also expanded on the things that brought me happiness even before I began this healing journey. I have always enjoyed entertaining friends and family, but now I can do this on my own without the arguments and stress of a toxic relationship dampening those events. It is a truly wonderful experience—a joyful one, even—in which I get to share my home (and newfound love of cooking!) with those most important to me.

Joy also presents itself to me when I am fortunate enough to observe others experiencing their own breakthroughs, growth, and learning. When one person in a group heals, everyone in the group can experience a mutual benefit of healing. And as each person raises their consciousness, the collective consciousness of the group also rises. There is significant power when a group of people comes together, and experiencing these moments really lights me up.

You will be most joyful when you live authentically, in the present, and in alignment with your soul's purpose. Let me break down each of these individually:

1. **Living your life as your true, authentic self** is critical to finding and maintaining joy. What does it mean to "live your truth"? That might sound hokey to you. It really just means following your heart and intuition and being yourself—not some version of yourself that you create in order to fit in with or please other people.

2. **Living in the present moment** was something I almost never did in my past and still struggle with to this day. My mind was constantly either dwelling on the past or worrying about or attempting to plan the future. Neither of these scenarios includes actually living in the present, which is the only point in time that we have any control over what happens. And the present is the only place where true joy resides.

3. **Living in alignment with your soul's purpose** was also a foreign concept to me until about five months after leaving my ex. We are all here to serve a purpose (or multiple purposes). Your soul chose this life you're living with a purpose in mind. When we are out of alignment with our purpose, we lack not only joy but also motivation and direction.

"The two most important days in your life are the day you are born and the day you find out why."

—MARK TWAIN—

For most of my life, I didn't know what my purpose was for being here. Then I discovered the coaching programs available through the Gay Man Thriving organization. I experienced joy in witnessing others' journeys and being able to provide others with insightful advice from my experience that could help them find their own happiness. I realized I felt more fulfillment in these conversations than anything else I'd ever done in my life. This journey of loving and being true to yourself has all sorts of amazing results.

> "If you want to find your true purpose in life, know this for certain: Your purpose will only be found in service to others, and in being connected to something far greater than your body/mind/ego."
>
> —DR. WAYNE DYER—

I do still have room for more joy in my life. Peace and confidence are two areas where I seek to improve. I definitely feel an increased level of both—as compared to where I was—but I want and need more of these, and I know that joy will be easier to feel when I find more peace and confidence.

It's not like a few months of healing was all it took for everything to be perfect. On the contrary, I believe we all have an eternal journey of continued growing, healing, and achieving higher levels of joy.

However, my introduction to joy has allowed me to realize that it's not something I want to give up. I'm never going back to my old way of being. Things are too good now, and I love myself too much to let that happen. And now that I've found it and vowed to keep it, things only continue to get better. Doesn't that sound nice?

—ACTIVITY—

Each morning for at least two weeks, write down ten things that bring you joy, happiness, and pleasure—as well as why these are good for you or why you're grateful for them. I also suggest the following:

1. Try to mix it up with simple stuff (e.g., chocolate ice cream) and bigger stuff (e.g., specific relationships, your spiritual connection to a higher power, etc.).
2. Try not to repeat items from one day to the next—or if you do, come up with different reasons for how they bring you joy, happiness, pleasure, and gratitude.
3. Hint: you don't have to stop at ten.

ACKNOWLEDGING YOUR VALUE

Let's talk about how you view your value as a human being, also known as your self-worth.

I have a history of discounting my accomplishments. I was quite gifted as a kid between academics and playing piano, but I took these things for granted because they came so easily to me. I just felt these were natural-born abilities, which to some extent they were. However, I never really celebrated those talents.

To this day, I've only just started to acknowledge and appreciate my gifts. Being around friends and family who call these things out definitely helps. It also helps to surround myself with people who are excited to celebrate my strengths and wins because they don't feel threatened by me.

I have a feeling you can relate to this. Have you downplayed the good things you've accomplished or your inherent qualities as a human being? Then it's time to do something about that! The first activity at the end of this section will allow you to identify some good things about yourself to celebrate. And I want you to really brag about yourself here. You don't have to worry about being boastful because only you will know what's on your list. If you're struggling to come up with a list, ask a trusted family member or friend (one you know will be happy to answer without feeling annoyed or jealous).

As I've only recently learned to do, I encourage you to really take in the moment when someone pays you a compliment. Don't shrug it off or tell the person they're wrong (either aloud or to yourself). Instead, accept the compliment with a simple, "Thank you." You are also not obligated to give a compliment in return. (If the other person expects this, their heart wasn't necessarily in the right place.) Automatically returning a compliment just because you received one takes some of the power away from the original compliment you received, and we've already discussed the dangers of people-pleasing.

> "How wonderful it is that nobody need wait a single moment before starting to improve the world."
>
> —ANNE FRANK—

Outside of those moments of receiving compliments, I would also encourage you to pay similar compliments to those you love more often. Do it with strangers, too! Again, it might feel awkward or uncomfortable at first—especially if these aren't exchanges you experience very often in these relationships. But who doesn't love a compliment?

Doing this will solidify a deeper bond in your relationships and often make someone's day. Telling people what you appreciate about them can go a long way.

At times or maybe even now, you may have felt a sense of worthlessness—an inability to come up with anything good to say about yourself. Maybe some close loved ones would say nice things about you that you didn't (or don't) believe.

I've been there. For me, it was really hard to believe positive things that others would say when the one person who meant the most to me not only didn't say those things but often said the opposite. I relied too much on the opinion of one person to really listen to others or notice how I felt about myself.

The journey of discovering, building, and maintaining a high level of self-worth is ongoing. Some of the big leaps we can take to achieve this include ending a toxic relationship, going to therapy, or beginning an exercise regimen.

One of the first major ways I acknowledged my value as an adult was changing jobs for the first time. I worked for my first company for nine years, during which I often worked eighty-hour weeks with disproportionate financial recognition for my efforts. Like many organizations, my company did not do a good job of taking care of the employees who grew up with the organization out of college and instead would reward mid-career hires with more money and seniority than their peers—regardless of actual talent.

Over the course of the last few years of my time there, I went through three separate full interview processes at different employers and was ultimately rejected each time. I allowed these rejections to impact my self-worth and decided to give up on trying to pursue a different job.

But those rejections were for the best. Finally, without seeking it, I was presented with an opportunity for 50 percent more pay and 50 percent less work than my then-current job, and I took it. (It was also more pay and less work than the other positions I had applied for and didn't get.) This was not an easy decision, given my loyalty to specific team members I left behind, but I realized—possibly for the first time—that I had to take care of myself first. And I haven't looked back. The environment at that first company was toxic. (Notice the parallels here to other types of relationships.)

The steps I took to look elsewhere and ultimately choose my own well-being were an example of the types of significant leaps you can take in acknowledging your self-worth. But it's also important to take small steps in that direction as well.

I could sit here and tell you that you're worthy of love and compliments, which would be true. But hearing this from other people (especially someone like me, whom you don't know) isn't going to do you any good. Instead, a belief of worthiness has to come from within yourself.

I encourage you to develop an ongoing practice of acknowledging your value. I've included a second activity at the end of this section to do just that, which might feel awkward or uncomfortable at first. I don't care—do it anyway. The point of this is for you to develop a sense of worthiness and pride in who you are and what you can do. And once you have developed that, continuing with the practice will help you maintain these feelings or even improve upon them.

Consistency is key. These measures won't work if you only try them for a few days and then give up. On the other hand, there's a good chance you'll find by doing activities like this on a daily basis (as I've done) that you start to view yourself in a significantly more positive light. And when that happens, as I've mentioned elsewhere in this book, everything else starts to fall more and more into place.

—ACTIVITY 1: ONE AND DONE—

Write fifteen to twenty gifts you have. This can include talents (e.g., cooking) or qualities (e.g., honesty).

Okay, you're not done after all—I also want you to set a reminder to revisit this list once a month or so to review what you've written (and add to it if more gifts come to mind).

—ACTIVITY 2: DAILY—

Before bed each night—every night for at least two weeks— answer the following prompts:

1. Which of my gifts did you use today? How did you use them?
2. Complete this sentence: "I am worthy of love and joy because . . ."
3. What intentions can you set for tomorrow to use your gifts for good?

IN CLOSING

You'll find true happiness and joy as you embark on the healing journey. Everyone's path is different and may include some combination of individual or group therapy, couples or family counseling, twelve-step programs, spirituality, mentorship, and coaching. I recommend prioritizing individual therapy for anyone healing from abuse or addiction. Therapy will also help those experiencing internal challenges like anxiety, depression, or battles with their sexuality or gender identity. Including techniques like hypnotherapy and breathwork will allow you to both discover the source of your thought and behavior patterns as well as let go of what no longer serves you.

Sitting with our feelings—and learning to express our emotions in healthy ways—allows us to heal and move on from the discomfort of negative emotions. Releasing those blocks makes room for happiness and joy, which stick around as constants and can coexist with temporary, uncomfortable emotions of sadness, anger, and fear.

Healing ourselves opens our hearts, removes our intimacy barriers, and allows us to invite love from other people. When we fully trust ourselves, we are able to trust others and create new levels of intimacy. And "intimacy" in this sense goes well beyond sex; it means a deep, meaningful emotional connection between two people.

By doing the work on ourselves, we can begin to enjoy the benefits of happy, healthy relationships with others.

—REFLECTION—

What steps can you take this week to begin (or continue) healing yourself?

HEALTHY RELATIONSHIPS WITH OTHERS

WHAT HEALTHY RELATIONSHIPS DO *NOT* LOOK LIKE

The phrase "you complete me" or "they complete me" irks me to no end. Fuck that—*I* complete me. *You* complete yourself. Or at least, that should be our goal. I feel so strongly about this concept that I even contemplated titling this book *I Complete Me.*

Other unhealthy mentalities with respect to romantic relationships include:

1. I need you.
2. I can't live without you.
3. I don't know what I'd do without you.

I believe the concept of one person completing another is complete bullshit. This can include phrases like "two halves making a whole" or "my other half" (or worse, "my better half"). It embodies the concept of codependency, which we've already explored as being unhealthy.

But that's the danger of entering into relationships when we haven't done the work on ourselves. If we don't have a good relationship with ourselves and we feel like we're missing something, we may look to a relationship with someone else to fill that gap.

HEALTHY RELATIONSHIPS WITH OTHERS

We fulfill our own destinies through self-exploration (working on ourselves, as we discussed in the last chapter); finding, creating, and maintaining our own happiness; and determining and seeking to achieve our goals. We don't need another person to do that. Relationships are meant to enhance our already fulfilling lives.

> "Perhaps the biggest mistake I've made in the past was that I believed love was about finding the right person. In reality, love is about becoming the right person. Don't look for the person you want to spend your life with. Become the person you want to spend your life with."
>
> —NEIL STRAUSS—

WHAT HEALTHY RELATIONSHIPS *DO* LOOK LIKE

Healthy relationships are based on interdependency instead of codependency. Both partners have established their individuality. Each person is fully complete on their own, without relying on another person or the relationship in order to feel complete.

Healthy relationships are about complementing one another, not completing each other.

When we have that healthy relationship with ourselves and are complete on our own, we attract another healthy, complete, fully independent person to us and can create something beautiful with that person. On the other hand, when we're missing something in the relationship with ourselves, we look for someone else to fill that gap, either consciously or subconsciously.

Relationships should be about enhancing our lives. Another person and the corresponding relationship can bring some wonderful aspects into our experience:

1. Connection—physical, emotional, mental, sexual, and spiritual
2. Laughter, enjoyment, and fun
3. Support, advice, and a listening ear
4. Inspiration and motivation for each other—just by nature of being yourself, loving yourself, and doing your own work
5. Introduction to new and exciting things (hobbies, interests, concepts, and ideas)
6. Different perspectives and opportunities for furthering your growth and learning

These are wonderful contributions to life, but there are many other components of life that we can (and should!) have, even without a partner. When we have a healthy relationship with ourselves, we have a full concept of our own identity and can experience fulfillment, happiness, and connection with ourselves and others.

LET'S COMPARE, SHALL WE?

So, what does interdependency entail? Well, remember all the unhealthy stuff we discussed in relation to codependency? It is the opposite of all that.

In codependent relationships, *two codependents become one*:

PERSON A	PERSON B
(Appears) independent	Dependent
Fears abandonment	Fears abandonment
Needs to be needed	Needs to be taken care of
Unhealthy boundaries	Unclear personal identity
Needs to control	Needs the other to take control

1. Each person gets bored with the other
2. Each person becomes more needy
3. One outgrows the other
4. They remain together through fear of abandonment or habit
5. Resentment builds
6. Fear grows
7. Boredom grows

Source: The Wellness Institute.

In interdependent relationships, *two independents share with each other*:

PERSON A	PERSON B
Independent	Independent
Secure within	Secure within
Has own job/profession	Has own job/profession
Has own friends	Has own friends
Has own interests	Has own interests

1. Both admire each other
2. Both challenge each other (in a loving, healthy way)
3. Both support each other
4. Both remain together by choice
5. Both continue to grow
6. Both become more self-confident

Source: The Wellness Institute

"Our boundaries embody
a foundational social paradox:
this is me and that is you and we are one."

—BRITT EAST—

In a codependent relationship, the two individuals share many common characteristics and behaviors, but the key differences lie in one person's need to be needed, need to control, and an inability to establish and maintain healthy boundaries. Meanwhile, the other person needs to be taken care of and has little to no individual identity.

On the other hand, interdependency involves two whole people coming together to create and maintain a healthy relationship. Each person has an individual identity that remains intact throughout the life of the relationship. Being together enhances each individual's life, but neither individual is dependent on the other for personal happiness, growth, or survival.

Realistically, then, what does that look like? The chart on the next page summarizes how those characteristics manifest in everyday life.

CHARACTERISTICS OF UNHEALTHY RELATIONSHIPS	CHARACTERISTICS OF HEALTHY RELATIONSHIPS
Dishonesty, including: • Sugar-coating (telling people what they want to hear versus need to hear) • Inauthenticity (feeling the need to hide some part of the self from the other) OR Disrespectful honesty (honest feedback delivered in an unkind way)	Respectful honesty and authenticity • Telling people what they need to hear versus want to hear (in a loving, respectful way) • Feeling comfortable to be your true self without hiding any aspects • Delivering feedback honestly, respectfully, and lovingly

"Say what you mean. Mean what you say.
Don't be mean when you say it."

—MERYL RUNION—

Disagreements • Involve fighting, screaming, or disrespect OR No disagreements (avoiding confrontation at all costs, always agreeing with the other even when you don't really agree)	Disagreements • Are welcome to occur • Happen in a loving, compassionate, respectful, and constructive manner that includes active listening
One-sided • One person benefits • Only one individual puts in the effort to maintain the relationship	Two-sided • Mutually beneficial • Both individuals put in effort to maintain the relationship

CHARACTERISTICS OF UNHEALTHY RELATIONSHIPS	CHARACTERISTICS OF HEALTHY RELATIONSHIPS
Lack of boundaries • Not saying no • Not speaking up when something doesn't sit right with you • Constantly acting as a therapist	Clear boundaries • Saying no when necessary • Speaking up in a loving manner when a boundary needs to be set or reinforced • Mutual support
Rescuing the other • Stifling the other's emotions • Fixing problems for the other • Providing advice without allowing the other to figure things out for themselves	Providing safe space • Allowing the other to feel whatever emotions come up • Providing support and a listening ear while allowing the other to fight their own battles
Anticipating the other's needs in order to receive love and avoid being hurt	Thoughtfully giving and allowing the other to ask for what they need and feeling free to do the same
Prioritizing the other's needs over your own needs	Mutually respecting the equality of each other's needs but taking care of your needs first so that you have the ability to meet the other's needs
One or both individuals are insecure • Relying on reassurance and validation • Constantly needing confidence boosts	Both individuals are secure • Each is confident in their identity and feel safe in the relationship • Compliments and validation are shared generously but are not required by either person

CHARACTERISTICS OF UNHEALTHY RELATIONSHIPS	CHARACTERISTICS OF HEALTHY RELATIONSHIPS
Jealousy of successes or using self-serving manipulation (e.g., "I know your networking event is really important for your career, but I don't feel like going. Let's stay home and cuddle instead—doesn't that sound so much nicer?")	Wanting what's best for each other and providing support and encouragement (e.g., in the example to the left, this could mean attending the networking event together or asking the other if they mind attending the event alone, still supporting and encouraging even when not physically present)
Gossip about other individuals whom both people know	Each person is respectful of others who are not present
Unconstructive, unsolicited criticism	Constructive, respectful feedback when appropriate and requested or invited
Unbalanced contributions to the relationship, household, and family life	Equitable contributions to the relationship, household, and family life
Enabling unhealthy behavior, such as: • Emotional behaviors described above • Physically unhealthy habits like drugs, alcohol, smoking, overeating, and undereating	Promoting healthy behavior • Providing support and a safe space to discuss unhealthy behaviors • Helping hold the person accountable to make healthy changes, but without accepting responsibility for their ultimate behavior

Right now, you might be thinking, "Well, damn—that's a lot. And my relationships don't come anywhere near to checking all the boxes in the 'healthy' column." First of all, that's okay—few relationships check all those boxes consistently with nothing from the "unhealthy" column ever showing up. All relationships are a work in progress. Secondly, this information is meant to guide you on what characteristics exist in a healthy relationship so that you can see how your current relationships overlay on the spectrum of unhealthy versus healthy.

We are all human and, therefore, imperfect. We can have healthy relationships, even if one or both individuals exhibit characteristics from the "unhealthy" column from time to time or have not evolved to fully embody the characteristics from the "healthy" column. For example, jealousy may occur once in a while, but it's important to recognize it as unhealthy and talk through it with the other person. Other people may struggle with all sorts of insecurities, but that's okay—as long as they don't become all-consuming. And again, it's important to communicate these struggles with unhealthy tendencies to our partners so they know what we're experiencing.

Healthy relationships are built on honest, open, and loving communication. They involve creating a safe space where each person can feel comfortable expressing their feelings—as opposed to an unhealthy environment, where expressing feelings leads to denial or defensiveness.

Our feelings are always valid, regardless of others' opinions or intentions. In the moment, someone may unintentionally upset you, which may cause a negative reaction from you. Afterward, it's certainly healthy to have a calm conversation about their intention as well as your (potentially unhealthy) reaction—but your feelings in the heat of the moment are valid. It's not okay for someone to suggest that you shouldn't feel a certain way.

And when I say, "Our feelings are always valid," that's a reminder to yourself, too. We shouldn't stifle our emotions because that's how unhealthy buildup occurs. Feelings are good and healthy to experience, but it's important to express them in a healthy way. I often have to correct my own self-talk from "I shouldn't be feeling this way" or "I don't want to feel this way" to "I accept how I feel." I remind myself to sit with that feeling, to examine it, and to learn what I need to learn. Remember—feelings exist to give us information.

Respect is another key component of a healthy relationship. We cannot expect two partners to agree on everything. Some romantic partners disagree often but can continue to thrive in the relationship because each person respects the other's viewpoint. The two may reach common ground or agree to disagree.

Some characteristics can exist in both unhealthy and healthy relationships, but there are important differences in how they present themselves.

For example, having fun is a common element of both unhealthy and healthy relationships. But how are you having fun? Are you having fun at someone else's expense (whether that someone is inside or outside the relationship)? Are you partaking in physically unhealthy activities on a regular basis (e.g., drinking, binge eating, doing drugs) *in order to* have fun? In healthy relationships, we can simply enjoy each other's company while doing fun, safe, and healthy activities.

Another example: helping people. Always a good thing, right? Well, let's think about it. If one person in a relationship is often doing more for the other than what feels good and with no ability (or safety) to say no or set limits, we're in unhealthy territory. On top of that, maybe the other person doesn't express gratitude or has guilt when asking for help. Or maybe there's a quid pro quo element to the help—expecting something to be done in exchange for that help.

In a healthy relationship, on the other hand, the help feels good to both individuals—free from guilt and expectation of something in return. The helper feels free to say no or set a limit in how the help is provided, which the asker respectfully acknowledges. And the asker expresses gratitude for whatever help the helper does provide.

There also needs to be a balance of how much help is requested and provided. Things are unbalanced when one individual is always the one asking for help and the other is always providing it. While, again, I don't believe a "tit for tat" mentality is healthy—there doesn't have to be an equal exchange of helping each other—we need to be careful that the relationship is two-sided, not one-sided.

A relationship is unhealthy when it regularly exhibits those characteristics from the examples provided here. And if one unhealthy characteristic happens regularly in a given relationship, I would venture to guess that other examples also occur in that same relationship. If you notice those patterns in any of your relationships, it's time for you to start setting boundaries and having important conversations about the health and future of your connection. And if these efforts are met with resistance, you may need to reevaluate whether it's appropriate and in your best interest to continue a relationship with that individual.

COMPATIBILITY IS A DIFFERENT TOPIC

Having a healthy relationship and having compatibility are two different things.

In theory, a relationship could exist between two healthy individuals whose personalities aren't compatible, but it probably wouldn't be very enjoyable. Some personalities just don't mesh well. Or maybe they mesh at an acceptable level but not to the extent that you want to spend your life with the other person. That's okay. *Just because two individuals are healthy doesn't mean they are meant for each other!*

Everyone has different strengths and weaknesses, too, which can bring balance to a relationship. As an example, one individual may generally exhibit healthy characteristics but still struggle with communicating their feelings (that would be me!). If this is you, too, being in a relationship with someone who effectively shares their feelings can be a really good thing and can help you grow in this area. We shouldn't *rely* on the other person to always bring out healthy characteristics in us, but they can be a good source of encouragement and inspiration just by being who they are.

When I talk about not using a relationship to complete or define us, I'm not talking about personality differences. For instance, maybe you're incredibly sociable and constantly on the go. Having someone who is "kind of boring" (likes to stay at home and not do much) might be good because it can bring balance to both of you—giving you some time to slow down and giving them the opportunity to spice up their life with some variety. Again, it's about complementing one another, not completing each other.

If we don't feel complete, the real issue comes down to love and happiness. An unhealthy mindset is not feeling loved unless someone else loves us or not being happy unless we are in a relationship. We have to find love for and happiness in ourselves first. Other people can enhance these feelings, but we have to have a solid foundation on our own.

LOVE OF SELF ALLOWS FOR SAFE AND HEALTHY LOVE OF OTHERS

Self-love, self-care, self-reflection, self-reliance, and self-empowerment are all essential components of an interdependent relationship. The whole point here is that each individual *could* live without the other, but instead they *choose* to be with each other—and continue to make this choice every day.

To some people, this concept may come across as self-centered or self-involved. (After all, the terms used in the previous paragraph are all *self-, self-, self-*!) In reality, it is entirely the opposite. As I've mentioned, there is a big difference between selfishness (or self-centeredness) and self-love. And I'll bring back that RuPaul quote again: "If you can't love yourself, how the hell are you gonna love somebody else?" This quote essentially captures everything I'm trying to say here: by putting yourself first and loving yourself first, you then have the capacity to fully love others.

Many characteristics of interdependent relationships can apply to both the relationship with the self and the relationship with another person:

CHARACTERISTIC	RELATIONSHIP WITH SELF	RELATIONSHIP WITH ANOTHER
Love and honor	I love and honor myself.	We love and honor each other.
Trust and safety	I trust and am safe with myself.	We trust each other and will make safe space for each other.
Honesty	I am honest with myself.	We are honest with each other.
Respect and admiration	I respect and admire myself.	We respect and admire each other.
Courage	I have courage to be myself with myself.	I have courage to be myself with my partner.
Inspiration and passion	I inspire myself and am passionate about my life.	We inspire each other and are passionate about our relationship.

CHARACTERISTIC	RELATIONSHIP WITH SELF	RELATIONSHIP WITH ANOTHER
Laughter and fun	I can laugh and have fun by myself.	We laugh and have fun together often.
Comfort	I can comfort myself.	We comfort each other.
Healing and forgiveness	I have my own healing journey in which I forgive myself and others when needed.	We heal our relationship when disagreements happen by forgiving each other when needed.
Health, strength, and balance on various levels of the relationship	I have a healthy, strong relationship with myself on an emotional, mental, physical, sexual, and spiritual level.	We have a healthy, strong relationship with each other on an emotional, mental, physical, sexual, and spiritual level.

Self-love is important to establish for ourselves as a precedent to having a healthy relationship. In an ideal but unrealistic world, I would say we do this work on ourselves to come to that place *before* even entering a relationship. However, oftentimes we learn some of our most important lessons by being in relationships—these lessons then teach us (sometimes by contrast) what a healthy, truly loving relationship should look like.

But because of the traumas and unhealthy relationships we may experience as children, we unintentionally attract unhealthy relationships as adults. Teenagers and young adults who feel unloved at home seek love from romantic partners and repeat those same patterns that left them feeling unloved in the first place. Individuals at that age are not yet emotionally intelligent or mature enough to understand their own feelings or how pain from the past may influence their lives in the now.

And by the time we reach an age when we do have the capacity to be emotionally intelligent and mature, many of us are still trapped in a cycle of unhealthy relationships—with other people as well as ourselves. Our fear of being alone, our lack of self-worth, and the underlying human need for connection lead us to "find ourselves" through relationships with others instead of through our relationship with ourselves.

These cycles can also continue even after ending those abusive, traumatic relationships in our lives. Many people realize how unhealthy their relationship is, manage to get out of it, but then attract another relationship that ends up with similar toxicity. Sometimes, the new relationship can be even worse than the original one because the universe is trying harder to make sure the lesson is learned.

This was one of my biggest fears as I began my healing journey—I did not want to repeat past mistakes and end up in another relationship like that. And the challenge with these relationships is that while there can be red flags along the way, the relationship itself might not be immediately painful—remember that cycle of abuse and manipulation? As I've said, abusers are very good at manipulating from the beginning, which is why the beginning of the relationship is often all sunshine, rainbows, and unicorns (okay, maybe not every instance is as gay as I just described). The gradual dissolving of the fantasy world is what makes it difficult to realize what is happening.

I didn't want to "waste" even six months of my life in a relationship like that, only to find out it was a repeat of what I experienced before. What I didn't understand was that doing the right work on myself would help prevent this from happening.

Ultimately, I didn't trust myself or my own judgment, so I needed to work on that, as well as heal and transform the relationship I had with myself. I've said it before: the relationships we attract are a direct reflection of the relationships we have with ourselves—so if we continue to abuse ourselves and don't do the work to heal old traumas and wounds, we will undoubtedly attract more abuse from others.

Knowing yourself at the core will keep you safe. *When you take care of yourself and are safe with yourself, you can be around others who haven't done the work on themselves and not be burdened by it.* And let's be real: most people haven't "done their work." That's one of the big reasons why doing your own work is so important—so you can feel okay and good even when people and things around you are going nutso.

Often, the most upsetting things that others say to us or about us are things that we believe to some degree. When we know these things aren't true, we can still feel safe when others are mean or rude or exhibit unhealthy behaviors because we know those words and actions aren't about

> "Do no harm,
> but take no shit."
>
> —MOÏRA FOWLEY-DOYLE—

us. That doesn't mean, however, that we tolerate this unacceptable behavior—we can and should still stand up for ourselves. But knowing ourselves allows us to avoid being triggered or upset by what others do and say.

This healthy relationship with and understanding of the self also allow us to attract new, healthy relationships. If we treat ourselves with love and respect, we will attract people who will do the same to us.

Raising our consciousness through these healing, learning, and growing processes also puts us in a new state of being. If we have a healthy relationship with ourselves, there is essentially no danger of attracting unhealthy relationships with others. We won't tolerate any unwelcome or abusive behavior or words from others. And often, those individuals will not even be on our radar once we're in that new state of being.

Therefore, now I can say with near certainty that I will never end up with another alcoholic or abuser in any type of close relationship in my life—as long as I continue to do the work of healing, growing, and loving myself. There's no room for it, nor would I tolerate the harmful aspects of those types of relationships. The same can be true for you.

DISAGREEMENTS AND "HARD WORK"

You can tell a lot about a couple by how they handle disagreements.

Disagreements will still occur in interdependent, healthy relationships. They are unavoidable because no two people think, feel, and act the same way. A relationship with no disagreements is likely not a healthy one—in that case, one or both partners are likely so conflict-averse that they suppress any differing opinions or feelings. This suppression will show up in unhealthy ways at some point.

So if disagreements show up in both healthy and unhealthy relationships, how can you tell where the relationship falls on the healthiness spectrum? The difference is in how the two people work through the disagreements.

In a healthy relationship, both individuals remain respectful, honest, and relatively calm—with both people listening to each other in an open and loving manner. And if one individual is disrespectful or dishonest, the other will feel safe enough to call them out on it. When this happens, the one at fault will accept personal responsibility for the unwanted behavior, apologize, and mean it. (To that, even if your relationship is relatively healthy, you might be thinking, "I wish!" I know, I know. But there is always room for improvement. In the meantime, remember that we're all imperfect and will continue making mistakes as we learn and grow. But awareness of how disagreements unfold in a healthy relationship is important.)

Active listening is a valuable approach to allow yourself and others to feel heard. It involves reflecting back to your partner what you hear to ensure you fully understand their thoughts and feelings—which shows them that you're really hearing them and making an effort to understand.

Healthy disagreements result in resolution or compromise and, ultimately, reconciliation if needed. In contrast, in unhealthy relationships, disagreements drag on and on without resolution and without a willingness to see each other's perspectives. Unhealthy disagreements can also escalate to the level of fighting, name-calling, and "low blows" (purposeful hurtfulness).

It takes practice to handle disagreements in a healthy manner, especially when old habits have shown the opposite. However, when two individuals truly want the best for each other and the relationship, they will both be willing to put forth the effort to make this happen.

Let's discuss for a bit about whether healthy relationships must require "hard work." I believe that *reasonable effort* is absolutely required to communicate, to learn and meet each other's needs, to respect each other's boundaries, to be willing to compromise and sacrifice (appropriately), and to remain respectful in heated disagreements without letting our triggers take over and lashing out at the other. This effort should be consistent and should be a top priority.

However, while this work may not always be easy, I also don't believe the level of difficulty should come anywhere near being painful or exhausting. We should put the same amount of work into a romantic partnership as we put into the relationship with ourselves. Both partners should want to make that effort for the other person, for themselves, and for the relationship. And the rewards reaped from doing the work should be well worth it.

Therefore, I believe we should all be careful when using the phrase, "Relationships are hard work." This can be confusing and misleading—as evidenced by my misunderstanding as a teenager that the "hard work" of my abusive relationship was normal and acceptable.

HEALTHY COMMUNICATION AND EXPRESSION

Communication is a critical component to all relationships. In fact, it is often the determining factor in whether a relationship succeeds or fails.

Many of us—myself included—hold back from communicating how we feel about things because we want to avoid confrontation. Sometimes we assume the other person knows how we feel—and assume we know how the other person feels—especially in long-term relationships where we know each other really well. No matter how well you think you know the other person, it's worth sharing your thoughts and feelings—you (or they) might be surprised by what you (or they) learn.

As a society, we also need to do more work on normalizing expressing emotion in a healthy way. *It is okay to cry!* Too often, people become uncomfortable when someone else becomes emotional. This discomfort rubs off on those around them and passes down to future generations who only continue the pattern.

Toxic masculinity teaches us that being emotional and vulnerable means being weak. I believe the exact opposite—*in vulnerability is exactly where strength lies*. It takes immense strength and courage to be vulnerable and freely express emotion, partly because of this ingrained fallacy of vulnerability equating with weakness that we have to overcome.

You don't necessarily have to exhibit as much vulnerability as publishing an entire book that contains your deepest, darkest secrets (*cough*), but you'll discover stronger connections with people when you begin to open up to one another about the internal struggles that each of you is facing.

Related to free expression of emotion is the concept of "toxic positivity," which is the idea that keeping positive at all costs is the right way to live your life. A bit of an extreme example would be if a loved one just died and your friend told you to think of all the good times you had with your loved one and not allow you to mourn the loss—either because they don't want you to feel pain or they are uncomfortable with your painful emotions.

Positivity has its place, and it's important, but it is not healthy to always revert to positivity, especially when it avoids feeling and processing difficult, challenging emotions. As we've discussed, feeling those uncomfortable feelings is critical to feeling the highest possible level of peace, love, and joy.

CONTINUED GROWTH THROUGH A HEALTHY RELATIONSHIP

If we do the work and maintain a high level of self-care and self-love, we will attract relationships with others who will respect, honor, and love us. Fortunately, that's exactly what happened for me.

In the months after I left my ex, I continued weekly therapy and joined a transformational coaching program through Gay Man Thriving. The opportunity to tackle both of these experiences simultaneously is, I believe, what helped me begin to heal and transform so quickly. I dedicated myself to self-improvement because I was not about to go back to where I had been. It was time for something different—and for that something to stick.

Five months after leaving my ex, I attended a live retreat with Gay Man Thriving and met the man who became my partner for ten months. It was completely unexpected for both of us. Initially, I had some trepidation because I still did not fully trust myself to choose the right partner for me. However, I learned quickly that I could trust my gut and see with my own eyes just how good he was for me.

Being in a healthy relationship was a game changer for me. I learned firsthand how it feels to be respected, heard, seen, appreciated, and truly loved. He supported me and provided a listening ear while still allowing me the personal space I needed to do my own healing and transformation, and I did the same for him. We shared experiences through the coaching program yet still had our own journeys. We inspired each other and challenged each other to be the best, truest version of ourselves.

In retrospect, I do believe we rushed into relationship status too quickly. We immediately jumped to being each other's partner and believing each other was "the one"—him (I believe) because he had never experienced a long-term relationship before, and me because there was such a stark difference between him and my abusive ex. While the attraction, connection, and love were real and quite strong, we could have taken things more slowly. However, I'm not sure that doing so would have changed how long we stayed together.

This isn't to say that fast-moving relationships are wrong for everyone—sometimes, "when you know, you know." However, I recognize now that I still had a significant amount of healing to do before I would be able to have and trust that gut feeling about someone.

We lived in different cities, which was a good thing given our tendency to rush things. If we had lived in the same city, I'm guessing we would have spent too much time together, which can easily become unhealthy. The long-distance aspect of the relationship allowed us to live our own lives. We talked almost every day but otherwise generally enjoyed our independence. And we both definitely looked forward to in-person visits.

As the relationship continued and natural difficulties arose, it was challenging for me to distinguish between triggers that reminded me of the past versus events that were truly upsetting in the moment. Fortunately, he was patient with me in this regard. We all bring history to relationships that must be considered and respected in our everyday interactions.

For example, learning how to be open to having disagreements was a challenge for me. For fifteen years, the slightest difference of opinion led to tension, bickering, or a full-on blow-up argument. The long-term impact of this was significant discomfort on my part anytime a disagreement occurred between my next partner and me. The trigger would cause my chest to tighten and breathing to become labored. My defenses would be up because I was ready to be attacked. I had to remind myself that it was okay to disagree and that two healthy adults can reach compromise or at least a respectful understanding of each other's opposing views.

Toward the end of those ten months, I started having more and more gut feelings that my heart was guiding me in a different direction. The discomfort I experienced from a few situations that occurred near the very end allowed me to realize where my heart had been guiding me for some time. Those uncomfortable situations were nothing like what I experienced in my fifteen-year relationship, but I experienced enough discomfort and a strong enough inner knowing that I knew our relationship status needed to change for both of our highest interests.

Looking back, I could have done a better job of more clearly communicating my feelings along the way when I had concerns. I had improved my transparency and honesty by leaps and bounds from my previous relationship because I did a better job of speaking up in the moment when something bothered me. However, I did not always follow those conversations through to resolution because they were uncomfortable and, by nature, I still try to avoid conflict whenever possible.

I still hesitated to communicate my feelings in the first place—not only because of how that had always backfired in my abusive relationship but also because of the ingrained belief from childhood that it wasn't safe for me to communicate my feelings without repercussions. Fortunately, being in a healthy relationship allowed me to gain more comfort and feel more safety with expressing myself—but I still have room for improvement in this area.

The end of our romantic relationship also brought a lesson and reminder to trust my gut, and had I not experienced an abusive relationship for fifteen years and done the work to heal and transform, I wouldn't have recognized the messages that my heart and body were sending me. They were subtle at first but continued to increase in intensity so that I would pay attention to them.

Those gut feelings contradicted certain arguments from my head, which centered on how generally good he was for me and how many "boxes he checked." He was loving, thoughtful, caring, patient, respectful, honest, funny, fun, open-minded, growth-oriented, financially stable, responsible, and lovable—all of which are qualities that are critical for any partner of mine. Still, my heart and gut said he wasn't for me any longer, and I knew I had to listen.

My codependent tendencies lingered especially at the end of the relationship—both immediately before and immediately after we broke up. I was afraid to end it, and then once I did, I questioned whether I made the right decision. In both cases, I felt my actions in deciding to end our partnership were responsible for his emotions. Having a cognitive understanding that only our own thoughts—not others' actions—determine our emotions was one thing; it was different to feel and know that on an emotional level.

Even through the toughest time of breaking up, we kept things respectful and honest. Not once in our relationship—including the breakup—did we scream at each other or intentionally hurt one another. I am proud of both of us in this regard.

For the vast majority of our relationship, I would say we fell in the "healthy" column of the chart earlier in this chapter. I still consider our relationship to be a healthy one even though some unhealthy characteristics popped up here and there. There are always opportunities for further growth and learning.

Our relationship wasn't perfect because there is no such thing as a perfect relationship. But it was pretty damn good.

My final lesson in this experience was that simply having a healthy relationship with someone doesn't mean it will last forever. And when it doesn't, *healthy relationships can have healthy endings, too.*

In our case, the relationship hasn't ended—it's just different. We concluded our romantic partnership on good terms and still enjoy a healthy friendship. Our relationship has changed how it looks, but I expect to continue enjoying and mutually benefiting from being in each other's lives.

THIS STUFF APPLIES TO OTHER RELATIONSHIPS, TOO

As a reminder, my message to you about relationships extends beyond romantic partnership and includes friendship, family, and professional relationships.

Similar to romantic relationships, I believe that there are varying degrees of healthiness in friendships. The charts from earlier in this chapter that summarize the characteristics of unhealthy and healthy relationships apply here as well, though they might look a little different.

What does "being a good friend" mean to you? Do you have a people-pleasing approach to these relationships? Saying yes when you want to say no? Avoiding disagreements at all costs? Being less than forthright to avoid hurt feelings? Remaining friends and keeping in contact out of obligation and simply because you have so much history with the person—when it's possible the relationship is no longer mutually beneficial? If your answer to any of these questions is yes, you may need to reevaluate your approach.

If you're anything like me, you may struggle with the idea of letting go of certain relationships out of obligation to continue them because of the amount of history and length of the relationship.

(*Red lights flash. An alarm buzzes loudly and repetitively and scares the shit out of you.*) Remember what I said about the sunk cost fallacy? Investing more time and energy in something simply because of how much time and energy you've invested up until that point is not a logical, valid reason. There are no badges or trophies for being loyal to someone who doesn't reciprocate your friendship in a healthy, valuable, mutually beneficial way.

Relationships are likely not mutually beneficial if one person is constantly a drain on the other—either by repeatedly asking for things, dragging the other down by complaining, or generally requiring too much attention. As with any good relationship, there needs to be a balance in the give and take, as well as in the energy exchanged. If one person consistently requires being built up with encouragement and positivity, it can become a significant burden on the other person doing all the work.

Sometimes, the group dynamic of a circle of friends can be toxic. If every gathering involves complaining about each other's lives and relationships with no subsequent material changes to make things better, there is little room for anyone in the group to grow. Gossip and trash talk about others outside of the group—or even inside the group—are also not healthy. Conflict within the group is often not dealt with in an honest, direct, or productive way. And alcohol or drugs only intensify insecurities and sensitivities to (and in) one another.

Healthy friendships are intended to raise each other up and allow for continued growth—not keep two (or more) individuals in an endless cycle of negativity and stagnancy.

On a more severe scale, unhealthy non-romantic relationships can also be abusive, manipulative, dramatic, and emotionally or mentally draining. If you question whether someone cares about you after repeated betrayal or uncomfortable interactions, it's time to reevaluate whether it's in your best interest to continue that relationship.

Friendships should be relatively effortless to maintain and navigate. They may require some effort to prioritize making time for one another or handle disagreements if personalities sometimes clash, but the effort should not be at a level that drains, frustrates, or worries you. We all have enough going on in our lives without having to deal with challenging friendships.

As for the obligation to maintain a familial relationship, I'm not suggesting you cut off all ties—unless it is toxic or abusive, in which case I refer you to the chapter on emotional abuse. Those same concepts would apply in this situation (even though that might become complicated with other family members in the mix). Outside of toxic situations, you can still have a relationship with these individuals, but it may need to be modified.

> "You can't change the people around you, but you can change the people around you."
>
> —UNKNOWN—

For both friends and family, there are often ways to limit your interaction with individuals if your relationship with them exhibits more unhealthy characteristics than you would like. No, that doesn't mean you have to march up to them and say, "I want to spend less time together."

But I've said this before, and I'll say it again: when you do the most loving thing for yourself, you give everyone around you exactly what they need. Therefore, if you limit your contact with these individuals for your own well-being, in the end, it will be better for them as well because you're living authentically and in alignment with the true you. Sharing an inauthentic version of yourself with others is beneficial to neither you nor them.

Limiting contact with challenging individuals in a professional environment can be trickier, depending on the situation with your job. Perhaps you have a supportive manager who can intervene or somehow help you navigate a difficult relationship. Maybe your manager *is* the problem relationship, in which case you might want to discuss with Human Resources. If you have multiple problem relationships at work, maybe this isn't the right environment for you. Ultimately, you have to decide if the job and pay are worth remaining in an environment with challenging, potentially toxic and draining relationships.

For the relationships you decide to continue despite challenges, it's important to discuss your concerns and establish boundaries. And again, if that conversation is met with disrespect or defensiveness, you may have your answer to whether you need to set limitations—or whether it's right to continue in that relationship at all. Ultimately, do what feels right for you.

LESSONS FROM THE UNIVERSE TO BUILD HEALTHY COMMUNITY

Opportunities for self-reflection and growth present themselves on all sorts of different levels. Some involve only yourself, some involve one other person or a few people, while others are on a much grander scale.

In addition to building healthy relationships with other individuals, we can also build healthy communities. The more people do their own work, the more opportunity exists for the creation and maintenance of healthy families, communities, and beyond. The healthiness of these larger groups is more difficult to maintain because it requires more than just one or two people doing the work on themselves.

We have no control over what other people do with their lives. It's up to us to do our own work in order to feel safe with ourselves, regardless of what happens around us. But doing that work on ourselves is also the best way for us to encourage others to do the same and ultimately make the world a better place.

> "Alone we can do so little; together we can do so much."
>
> —HELEN KELLER—

When multiple people who are doing their own work come together, they can create, build, maintain, and grow a thriving community that serves them and those outside the community in beautiful, creative, helpful, and loving ways.

I think we can all agree that the year 2020 was a challenging and unusual time with the COVID-19 pandemic. It was something that affected every individual in one way or another. But in spite of the many frustrations and difficulties associated with it, I viewed it as a message and an opportunity. From the start of lockdown, I viewed the experience as the universe's way of giving us an opportunity to self-reflect and look inward.

And I feel it is no coincidence that possibly the most attention toward racism and white privilege that we've had in a long time has occurred in the midst of the global pandemic. The message and opportunity for both of these situations were the same: the universe was telling us that what we've been doing up until this point—how we treat ourselves and others—has not been working, and things need to change.

Quarantine was an opportunity to take a deeper look at ourselves and our at-home life and improve or completely change our situation. The protests were and have been an opportunity to take a deeper look at how we treat those around us, how our system has been built, and what we can do to make things better.

I am embarrassed to admit that it took until 2020 (thirty-three years) for me to wake up and recognize just how significant of a problem racism is, acknowledge my privilege, and start to take active steps to (finally) do my part. Initially, I felt significant guilt about this delay, but I've since realized (without absolving myself of my prior ignorance and indifference) that less than one year prior to that, I was so unhappy, trapped, and absent from my own life that there was no way I could tune into the world around me. Now that I've released a significant amount of pain from my past and opened my heart, I am freer to empathize more easily with those around me.

I expect many people are unable to recognize the problems with how they view and treat other people because they are so focused on and engulfed in their own unhappiness. Think about the public comment threads on social media, for example. I believe that much of the polarity, injustice, inequality, disrespect, and anger that occur among individuals could be reduced or eliminated if we all did this important work on ourselves.

People often ask what they can do to make the world a better place. While there are all sorts of opportunities for activism, charity work, and other forms of directly helping others—all of which I strongly encourage—one of the best ways to positively impact the world around us is to develop and maintain a healthy, loving relationship with ourselves. I'll say this one last time: when we do the most loving thing for ourselves, we, in turn, give everyone around us exactly what they need. That includes *literally* everyone—not just the people we immediately encounter in our lives. There is a ripple effect that expands outward from person to person when we show up with love for ourselves and others.

> "Whatever affects one directly, affects all indirectly. I can never be what I ought to be until you are what you ought to be. This is the interrelated structure of reality."
>
> —MARTIN LUTHER KING, JR.—

IN CLOSING

Interdependency essentially involves two (or more) complete, healthy individuals coming together in a loving, supportive relationship in which they both choose to participate but do not need for their survival, depend on for their livelihood, or use to define themselves as individuals. (Hint: most pop songs do not provide helpful guidance in what healthy relationships look like.)

Each individual does their own work when it comes to the discovery and journey of the self—including growing, learning, and healing. The partnership includes support and encouragement along that journey, but each person is ultimately responsible for themselves.

"The greatest gift you can give to somebody is your own personal development.

I used to say, 'If you will take care of me, I will take care of you.'

Now I say, 'I will take care of me for you, if you will take care of you for me.'"

—JIM ROHN—

We must remember that no one—including ourselves—is perfect. We are all human. Therefore, mistakes will happen. More than likely, unhealthy moments will happen from time to time because we all carry shit from our past into the relationships we have now. This is where the importance of communication comes in. Honesty and transparency are critical to reaching common ground and finding that sweet spot that works for both (or all) individuals in the relationship.

By doing the work on ourselves, we can recognize what is healthy and safe for ourselves and what is not. When something isn't right for us, it's our responsibility to set healthy boundaries and stick to them—and in some cases, we may need to reevaluate relationships entirely. *Keep in mind that everyone has to make their own choices about what healthy boundaries mean for them—this can differ from person to person, and our own boundaries will also evolve over time. Boundaries are neither universal nor stagnant.*

All of this also applies to the relationship we have with our community and the world around us. The greatest gift we can give the world is doing the inner work to develop and maintain a healthy relationship with ourselves. In doing so, the snowball effect of our interactions with other people will continue expanding outward to positively impact all of humanity.

—REFLECTION—

Consider your top five to ten relationships—those to whom you feel closest or with whom you spend the most time.

1. Where do these relationships fall on the spectrum of healthy vs. unhealthy? What unhealthy characteristics exist in each relationship?
2. What boundaries need to be set, conversations need to occur, or approaches need to change?
3. What strengths from one relationship can you apply to other relationships?

CONCLUSION

A HEALTHY ME ALLOWS FOR A HAPPY WE

The "Happy We" portion of my book title has a twofold meaning: the "we" in a one-on-one relationship as well as the collective "we" of humanity. We as individuals have the power to create and maintain happy relationships with other people and make the world a happier place.

But in order to do that, first comes a "Healthy Me"—because it all starts with ourselves. A truly "happy we" is impossible without a "healthy me." There are different versions of happiness that exist because some people (my old self included) don't know any better; they don't know what true happiness looks like. Doing the inner work on ourselves is the key to happy relationships with other people and to bettering our communities and the world around us.

However, an important aspect of the heading above is that a healthy relationship with the self *allows for* happy relationships with others—but does not necessarily guarantee it. We can't control the words or actions of others. We can feel safe with ourselves regardless of what's happening around us—but if someone begins treating us in an unhealthy way that doesn't feel right, it's our responsibility to either set boundaries and stick to them or reevaluate the relationship status altogether.

The process of maintaining a healthy relationship with ourselves is ongoing. The work is never done, but it does get easier. Trust me—it can be really hard at first, when healing from years of pain and trauma. But after a while, it becomes second nature. And life becomes fantastic.

FROM VICTIM TO HERO

I am not a victim. I was never a victim, but I definitely perceived myself to be one for the longest time. *Victim mentality makes us believe that things happen to us instead of happening for us.* I felt I had no control over my own life. I didn't realize that only I had the power to begin making changes to improve my life and find happiness.

You are also not a victim. Victimhood implies that a person is helpless and can't do anything about their circumstances. While you may have been through some shit, too, I hope the message in this book is loud and clear: *you can take and maintain control of your own life.* You have the power to make your life amazing. We all have that power.

I am not a victim. However, I am a survivor. And I am both proud of and humbled by that.

In the middle of my healing journey, I saw a friend's post on social media about meeting his hero, which got me thinking about who my hero was. Without much hesitation, I realized and said to myself, "You know what? I'm my own damn hero."

Remember what I said in the introduction? We are all the protagonists of our own stories, but we may not necessarily be the heroes of our own stories. Doing this work on myself allowed me to get there. We can get to a place where we are our own biggest cheerleaders, our own biggest advocates, and our own biggest

"I hope culturally we can continue to normalize the idea that being a survivor is so much more common than anyone realizes and we all deserve to be heard, but more importantly are deserving of a recovery full of love, laughter, and light."

—JONATHAN VAN NESS—

inspirations. It just requires doing the work I've described throughout this book.

And we can be our own best friends, too. Sure, it's fun to have inside jokes and things to bond over with people, but it's also kind of fun to have some things just to ourselves. Maybe you enjoy something that no one else you know enjoys—and that's really cool. Appreciate your uniqueness. Take yourself on dates! We don't have to share everything with someone. Some things can just be things for us to enjoy on our own—inside jokes and interests are reasons to be your own best friend. *You are the only person who likes everything you like and has all your same interests.*

Having a strong, healthy relationship with ourselves allows us to have strong, healthy relationships with others. Get comfortable being by yourself. Get to know yourself inside and out. Be your own best friend. Be your own hero. You might be surprised what kind of positive impact this has on your other relationships as well.

NEW BEGINNINGS: SETTING AN EXAMPLE

Life is beautiful, exciting, and full of joy when we keep up on doing this work. When we prioritize growth, healing, and self-love, the whole new world that opens up for us is amazing.

One challenge we can experience in the process of this "up-leveling" is wanting to take our loved ones with us on the same journey. Once we know how good life is, we want those closest to us—and everyone else—to be as happy as we are. We come to realize that if everyone were this happy, the world would be a much safer, more peaceful, and more loving place.

I often have to remind myself that other people's journeys are not mine to take for them. I could overload my friends and family with everything I've learned, but it's not going to do them any good if they aren't ready to hear the message. Plus, too much encouragement and pushing can border on that rescuing aspect of codependency.

Another challenge we may face is having loved ones who begin a journey of healing and growth but reach a point where they are satisfied and no longer continue doing their work. This runs the danger of their falling back on old patterns and certainly impedes their ability to continue growing. And that is their choice. But it may or may not be for you.

By continuing down the growth path, you'll find more opportunities, achieve higher levels of happiness, and discover that the best is yet to come. But you may also find along the way that certain relationships no longer serve you—and that is okay. We can't force people to continue growing, just like we can't force them to start growing in the first place.

> "Just because it's the best you've ever had doesn't mean it has to be the best you'll ever get."
>
> —ANDREW SARTORY—

The best form of encouragement we can provide is to simply live our best lives in order to exemplify for others what it looks and feels like.

Think of it like a bridge that crosses over rough waters in the middle of the woods. At one end is where you are today, before starting the healing journey. At the other end is the destination of peace, love, joy, and happiness. The bridge represents doing the work. You walk along the path with your loved one and get to the bridge. You can cross the bridge yourself and get to the other side, but you can't do your loved one's walking for them. You can wave to them from the other end and encourage them to join you, but ultimately, it's up to them to take those steps across the bridge.[9]

This book has been my attempt to wave at you from the other side and welcome you to join me. I've shared my story to help you recognize what's working or not working in your life. I've explained what things look like once the healing journey begins. And I've encouraged you to take those steps across the bridge. But I can't take the journey for you—that's up to you.

---

9. Melody Beattie, "Letting Go of Those Not in Recovery." September 6, 2020, https://melodybeattie.com/letting-go-not-recovery.

LOOKING INWARD TO EXPAND OUTWARD

Now that you're almost finished with this text, let's revisit some questions from the beginning:

1. Are you happy?
2. If not, can you admit why you aren't happy? What (or who) is keeping you from being happy?
3. Would the eight-year-old version of yourself be proud, happy, and excited to become who you are now as an adult?
4. Are you really okay settling for unhappiness? Or do you want to finally do something about it—and make that eight-year-old proud, happy, and excited to become you?

Maybe your answers have changed between that first chapter and this last chapter—and maybe not. That's okay. These questions are still important to consider if you want to be happy.

Now let's recap what to do if you don't like your answers to the above questions:

1. **Examine your closest relationships.** Are any of them particularly challenging or utterly unbearable? If yes, you've got to make some changes—either set boundaries or end the relationship. Otherwise, your misery will continue. (Note: this is only step 1 if you have relationships that require significant changes.)
2. **Examine your relationship with yourself.** How do you talk to yourself? Do you understand the various cues from your mind, body, and soul in a given day? How do you react to stressful or painful situations? How do you feel just sitting by yourself?
3. **Get your ass into therapy.** (I *may* have mentioned this a time or two throughout the book.) Find a therapist with whom you have good rapport and who challenges you in ways that you can heal, increase your awareness, and have a better understanding of and relationship with yourself.
4. **Feel your feelings.** Sit with them. Don't push them down because they'll come back up eventually. Ask your therapist for help with this process—then you can start doing it on your own. *Repeat this step as needed. It will come up often.*

5. **Revisit your relationship with yourself.** What can you do to bring yourself happiness and joy? How can you treat yourself with more gentleness, patience, and love—the same way you treat others? How do your methods of self-care and continued growth align with your highest good?

6. **Revisit your relationships with others.** How can you employ healthy changes to improve your interactions with others and how you feel about those relationships?

7. **Surround yourself with other people who also prioritize their growth, healing, and happiness.** This doesn't mean you have to let go of everyone who doesn't fit the bill, but you should find (or build) a network of like-minded individuals as well. This can be in person, online, or a combination of both. We are stronger and better together.

8. **Remember that you are not alone.** I poured my guts into this book to help serve as a reminder of this for you. More than likely, others have also experienced whatever you are going through or have gone through. Shared experiences can be a powerful way to connect with others—all the more reason to create that network of trustworthy people that I describe above.

9. **Employ daily practices that support growth, presence, and a healthy relationship with yourself.** Some approaches that work for me include:
    -   Gratitude journaling: write three to five statements per day of people or things for which you are grateful, as well as *why* you are grateful for them. It is impossible to be in a state of victimhood or anger when we are in a state of gratitude. I find it particularly impactful to express gratitude for any current challenges because I know they always have lessons to teach me.
    -   Meditation: set aside at least five minutes per day for yourself to do this. Meditation teaches us how to be present and helps decrease anxiety. For additional information, see the back of this book.
    -   Affirmations: write and vocalize positive statements about yourself, like "I am strong, confident, and powerful" and "I love myself." It is critical to feel at least some truth behind these statements, or they won't really do you much good. If

you don't believe what you're writing or saying, imagine what it would feel like to believe those statements—and really feel into that emotion. I have written my statements on Post-it notes that I stuck to my bathroom mirror and read to myself aloud while looking myself in the eye.

10. **Share what you've learned.** I believe that the universe hands us our biggest challenges for a reason. Once we grow and learn from them, it's our responsibility to humankind to share those lessons with others. I expect that any individual's biggest challenges have a lot to do with that individual's main purpose for this life.

> "The hand of challenges we've been dealt is actually exactly what we need to reach joy and happiness."
>
> —JAMI CHRISTINE—

11. **Set an example for others.** This is the most effective way of sharing what we've learned. Teaching lessons about the challenges we've had can be helpful, but showing other people what it's like to heal and be happy will better encourage them to take their own journeys.

As you can see, this list is a combination of inward reflection and outward application. The order I've listed them in is intentional, though you may be able to mix them up a bit (and certainly repeat steps as needed). By first tackling the inward reflections and independent actions, you can examine the current state of your life and determine what's working for you and what's not—while still accepting where you currently are. From there, you can expand outward to apply that self-love and self-acceptance to your relationships with other people.

Before we can connect more deeply and healthily with others, before we can make a significant difference in the world, we have to take a long, hard look at ourselves. Improve our relationship with the self. Take care of the self. Get help. Heal.

And from there, everything else starts to open up. Things get easier. Life feels more fulfilling and energizing. We discover things about ourselves and those around us that we didn't know existed. We find purpose. We not only transform ourselves but also play our part in transforming our relationships and the world around us. We feel freedom, peace, and joy. We are happy.

RESOURCES

NATIONAL DOMESTIC VIOLENCE HOTLINE

1. By phone: 1-800-799-SAFE (7233)
2. By chat: thehotline.org

This hotline is for those suffering from not only physical abuse but also emotional, sexual, mental, and financial abuse—and for those who are questioning whether their relationships are abusive. Advocates are available 24/7/365 to discuss your situation and help you determine if your relationship might be abusive—and if so, what you can do to be safe and happy.

SUPPORT GROUPS

1. "Living with Narcissist Emotional Abuse"—This Facebook group is dedicated to supporting victims and survivors of the emotional abuse experienced from living with a narcissist, sociopath, or psychopath. Many group members have a narcissistic partner or ex-partner, but many others have narcissistic parents, children, siblings, friends, coworkers, etc. The group is private, so your Facebook friends will not be able to see your membership or participation.

2. Al-Anon Family Groups—http://al-anon.org—This group provides help and hope for families and friends of alcoholics. Depending on where you live, there are likely several groups and daily meetings available in your area. Meetings are traditionally held in person, but this has evolved to include online meetings (depending on the group) given the COVID-19 pandemic. Note that every group has a different look and feel, so it's important to test out different groups to find the right fit.

I am not exaggerating when I say that these two groups, coupled with individual therapy, saved my life during my darkest, most difficult hours.

Other groups similar to Al-Anon exist for more specific issues, including S-Anon (for codependents of sex addicts) and Codependents Anonymous (CODA). I have not attended these groups myself.

BOOKS

1. *Psychopath Free* and *Whole Again* by Jackson Mackenzie—Both books are about healing from abuse from relationships with narcissists, sociopaths, and psychopaths. They should be read in the order listed; *Psychopath Free* goes into greater detail about what to expect from being in the relationship as well as the immediate aftermath, while *Whole Again* supports the experience after having been out of the relationship for some time.

2. *How Al-Anon Works for Families & Friends of Alcoholics* (the "blue book")—This book provides the foundational teachings of Al-Anon and initial guidance on how to approach relationships with alcoholics.

3. *Codependent No More* and *Beyond Codependency* by Melody Beattie—Their respective subtitles (*How to Stop Controlling Others and Start Caring for Yourself* and *And Getting Better All the Time*) speak for what's covered in these. They should be read in the order listed. I recommend these books for anyone struggling with an alcoholic loved one and those who struggle with addiction themselves.

4. *Loving What Is* by Byron Katie—This book includes examples of back-and-forth discussions between Byron Katie and various

individuals doing "The Work" (as coined by Byron Katie). The examples allow us to accept the truth of reality and let go of people and things that are out of our control.

MEDITATION OPTIONS

1. Mobile applications—My favorites are Head Space, Calm, and Insight Timer. These are great for guided mediations. There are free and paid versions of the apps.
2. YouTube—My go-to meditation style now is to pull up a "video" of meditation music and sit in otherwise silence. YouTube has plenty of guided meditations, too.

ACKNOWLEDGMENTS

To Azul, it's difficult to summarize my gratitude in a sentence or two. Simply put, this book would not be where it is today without the love, insight, inspiration, support, encouragement, and friendship from you and Steve.

To Emily and Kim, for managing my editing and publishing process in a way that I felt safe to let go. And to Catherine, McKell, Lisa, Jessica, and Kaitlin, for helping shape the book into this final product. Your creative ideas along the way made me feel even prouder to share this book with the world.

To Pam, for holding safe space for me—and playing a critical role in saving my life—during my darkest days. I am forever grateful to both you and Erick for guiding my healing journey in a way that I feel reborn.

To Andrew and Zach, for designing and leading coaching programs that launched my healing and transformation into hyper speed. Plus, without these programs and my friendship with you, the idea for this book would have never materialized.

I have multiple families to thank: my biological family (including my loving parents), work family, friend family (or "Framily"), PTI (group therapy) family, Authors Who Lead family, and Gay Man Thriving family. I appreciate all of you for providing love and community for me to grow, learn, and transform—all while having fun, too.

To Jessica, for being the first person to read a completed draft of my manuscript. Thank you for providing the safe space for me to share my story. Your insights and suggestions were instrumental in transforming the book into what it has become.

To Michael and George, for providing helpful, constructive, and encouraging feedback early in the process.

To Jami, Julia, Heather, and Kim, for providing important suggestions that ultimately helped shape the final product, as well as insights related to your own experiences with unhealthy and healthy relationships. And to all four of you, for being some of the biggest sources of support and encouragement since my transformation began. Your independence and approach to life inspire me.

To my ex-husband, for teaching me what an unhealthy relationship looks like, with another and with myself. Without this experience that we shared, I wouldn't be the man I am today. And this book would not exist.

To Rob, for showing me what a healthy partnership looks like—and for your ongoing support and encouragement during the writing process. You will always hold a special place in my heart.

And to Peachy and Joey, my moral support who sat next to me on the couch as I wrote this entire book—even though they were asleep most of the time (and often snoring).

Finally, I want to acknowledge myself. I poured my heart and soul into this piece. I have bared my soul to you, the reader, in the hopes that it helps you transform your own life.

ABOUT THE AUTHOR

Ted Smith is committed to helping others find and maintain happiness through healthy relationships with themselves and others. In his spare time, he enjoys playing piano, exploring spirituality and personal growth, and spending time with friends and family (outside of global pandemics). He lives in St. Louis, Missouri, with his two cats, Peachy and Joey.

YOUR THOUGHTS
ARE APPRECIATED

What did you think of this book? I would appreciate your feedback on what helped you most, how you could relate, questions you have, and what you would like to see in future books.

Connect with me directly via email at ted@tedsmith.life.

Visit http://linktr.ee/tedsmith.life to connect with me in other ways:

1. Subscribe to my email list
2. Follow me on Instagram and Facebook
3. Listen to my recent podcast appearances

If you enjoyed this book and found it helpful, please leave a review on Amazon.